LETTER of the Week

The Complete Alphabet Book of Projects and Activities

Editors:
Debbie Blaylock
Lynn Coble
Amanda Wheeler

Written by
Lucia Kemp Henry

Contributing writer:
Amanda Wheeler

Contributing illustrator:
Cathy Spangler

Cover artist:
Terri Anderson Lawson

www.themailbox.com

©1993 The Mailbox® Books
All rights reserved.
ISBN10 #1-56234-095-6 • ISBN13 #978-156234-095-7

Printed in the United States
20 19 18 17 16 15

HPS 243173

Table of Contents

About This Book

Letter Of The Week *is a collection of 26 units, one for each letter of the alphabet. Each letter unit contains an art project, a cut-and-paste project, a creative-writing booklet page, a literature selection and accompanying activities, a recipe, a song, a fingerplay, and extension activities.*

How To Use This Book

Alphabet Booklet Pages

Each letter unit contains a booklet page for students to complete with their own art and dictated or written story ideas. As each youngster completes the booklet pages, save them to compile into a personalized alphabet book. A book cover pattern is included on page 187 to add a finishing touch to each youngster's book. If you do not wish to make alphabet books, use each booklet page as a letter review/creative-writing activity sheet.

Award Certificate: page 186

Reproduce this pattern page on white or colored paper, providing one award for each child. Fill in the blank spaces on each award and embellish it with foil or sticker stars, if desired. Staple each child's award to the end of his completed alphabet book.

Alphabet Book Cover: page 187

Reproduce the pattern page on white construction paper, providing one book cover for each child. Let each child decorate her cover with sponge-printed letters, crayon-drawn letters, stamped letters, or letter stickers. Use the completed page as a book cover for each child's personal alphabet book.

Alphabet Character Clip Art: pages 188–192

These pages contain ready-to-use clip art for all of the alphabet characters used in the book. Reproduce the characters as desired for the following possible uses:

Enlarge the designs
  • for 8" x 10" shape booklet covers
  • for large bulletin-board characters

Reduce the designs
  • to embellish take-home notes or newsletters
  • to glue onto small flash cards
  • to glue onto construction-paper bookmarks

Use the designs as shown for
  • student awards
  • nametags
  • counting activities
  • letter-to-picture matching activities

A is for apple

An apple activity a day will earn you an A!

Apple Fingerplay

Five little apples lying on the floor.
I'll roll one away, and that leaves four.
(Make rolling motion with arms.)

Four little apples hanging on a tree.
I'll pick one off, and that leaves three.
(Pick an imaginary apple.)

Three little apples, I know what to do!
I'll put one in my pocket, and that leaves two.
(Pretend to put apple in pocket.)

Two little apples sitting in the sun.
I'll pick one up, and that leaves one.
(Pretend to pick apple up off the floor.)

One little apple waiting in my lunch.
I'll eat it up with a crunch, crunch, crunch!
(Pretend to take a big bite!)

"Apple, Apple, On The Tree"

Sing this song to the tune of "Twinkle, Twinkle, Little Star."

Apple, apple, on the tree,
I know you are good for me.
You are fun to munch and crunch
For a snack or in my lunch.
Apple, apple, on the tree,
I know you are good for me!

The Caterpillar Ate The Apple

Use the *A* booklet page on page 6 as an individual worksheet or complete the page and save it for each child to compile an individualized alphabet book. Have each child trace and write each letter. Write each child's dictation to complete the sentence in the space provided.

Appetizing Applesauce

Delight your children by preparing applesauce in your classroom. Peel, core, and slice two pounds of cooking apples. In a heavy pot, gently simmer apples in 1/3 cup of water. Simmer covered until apples are tender. Remove pot from heat and mash apples with a potato masher. Applesauce will be slightly chunky. Add a small amount of sugar, about 1/3 cup, to sweeten. Add cinnamon to taste. Stir well and serve warm. You may be surprised by the number of students who have never tasted homemade applesauce.

The Apple Tree Game

Reproduce the apple tree game pattern on page 10 on tagboard, providing one pattern for each child. Have each child color the upper portion of his game. Cut away the bottom portion and cut out each apple. To play the game, look at the picture on each apple, say its name, and place it on the tree.

A Is For Apples

Aa—Apple Cut-And-Paste Project

Reproduce the apple cover pattern on page 7 on red construction paper. Reproduce the patterns on page 9 on white construction paper. Reproduce the back pattern on page 8 on red construction paper. Have each student color a caterpillar, stem, and leaf, and glue them to the cut-out apple cover as shown in illustration A. Fold the cover and back along the center fold lines. Lay the cover face-down. Cut out the apple center and glue it to the back of the right side of the apple cover. Glue the back of the caterpillar side of the cover to the left side of the back, placing glue only where indicated to form a pocket (see B). Have your youngsters color and cut out the picture cards, placing them in the apple pocket for storage. To play the game, have your students put the *A* picture cards on the squares inside the apple.

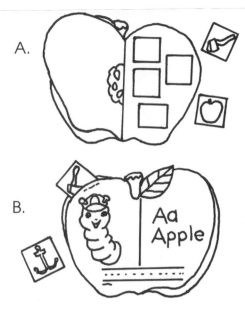

A.

B.

Johnny Appleseed by Steven Kellogg

- After reading the story, ask your youngsters to imagine that they have planted an apple seed. Have them dictate several steps to describe how their apple seed grows into a tree. Copy those sentences on lined paper. Title each story "[child's name] Appleseed." Ask each child to illustrate his written ideas. Hang each child's work on a large bulletin-board apple tree.

- Since Johnny Appleseed planted lots of apple trees, all of the resulting apples could make lots of "apple-icious" treats. Have your youngsters brainstorm a list of apple dishes. Write the list on chart paper. Let youngsters take turns circling all of the *A*s in the list with a red marker.

Additional Appealing Apple Tales

An Apple A Day by Judi Barrett
Apples, How They Grow by Bruce McMillan
The Seasons Of Arnold's Apple Tree by Gail Gibbons
The Apple by Dick Bruna
Applebet: An ABC by Clyde Watson

More Apple And A Activities

- Use a class circle discussion to help students think of other items that begin with the letter *A*. Have each child draw and color one of the items discussed. Display the students' work on a bulletin board titled "Apples Aren't Alone."

- Display a box of items in your room that begin with the letter *A*. Encourage your students to bring items to add to the box and use these items to reinforce the letter *A* by saying, "I wonder what *A* items we have in our box today?" Allow new items to be introduced by the owners.

- Serve alphabet soup and search for the letter *A*.

- Have students cut from magazines and bring in pictures of items that begin with *A*. Display the pictures on a large cutout of an apple titled "*A* Is All Around Us."

- Compare varieties of apples (such as McIntosh, Delicious, Golden Delicious, and Granny Smith) for size, color, and shape. Have students arrange the apples in descending order using the words *largest, smallest, larger than,* and *smaller than.*

- Explain to the children that apples have two seed patterns inside according to how they are cut. Cut an apple in half from top to bottom to reveal the oval pattern in the center. Cut another apple from side to side to reveal the star-shaped pattern.

- Have students hypothesize which color of apple has the most seeds. Cut each color of apple in half, dig out the seeds, and have a student count them. Record your findings on a large paper apple.

Apple

The caterpillar
ate the apple.

He ate it and said,

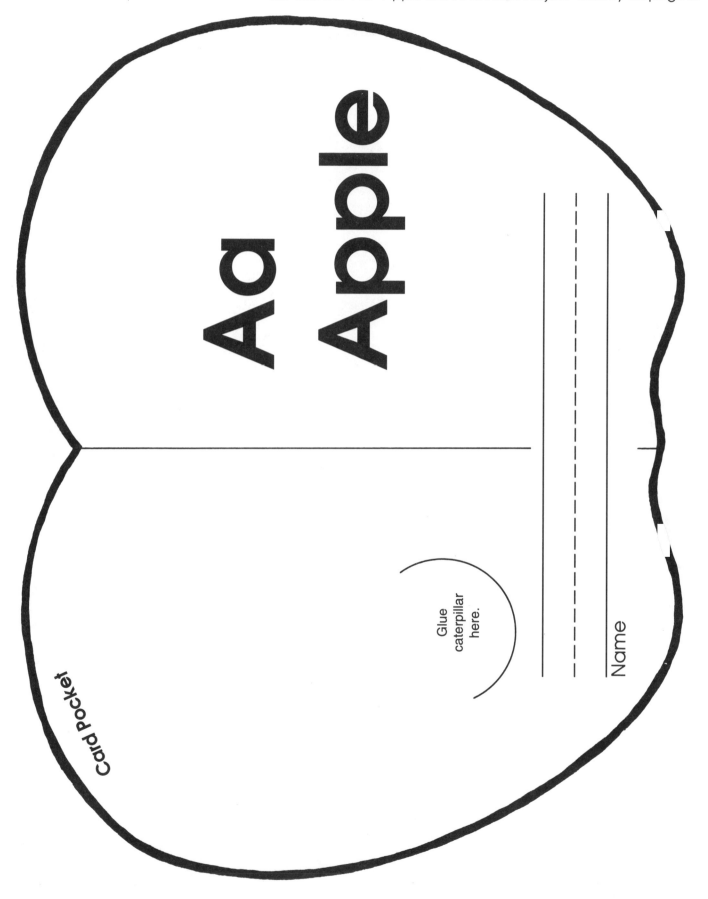

Aa
Apple

Glue
caterpillar
here.

Name

Card Pocket

Pattern
Back

Use with the "*Aa*—Apple Cut-And-Paste Project" activity on page 5.

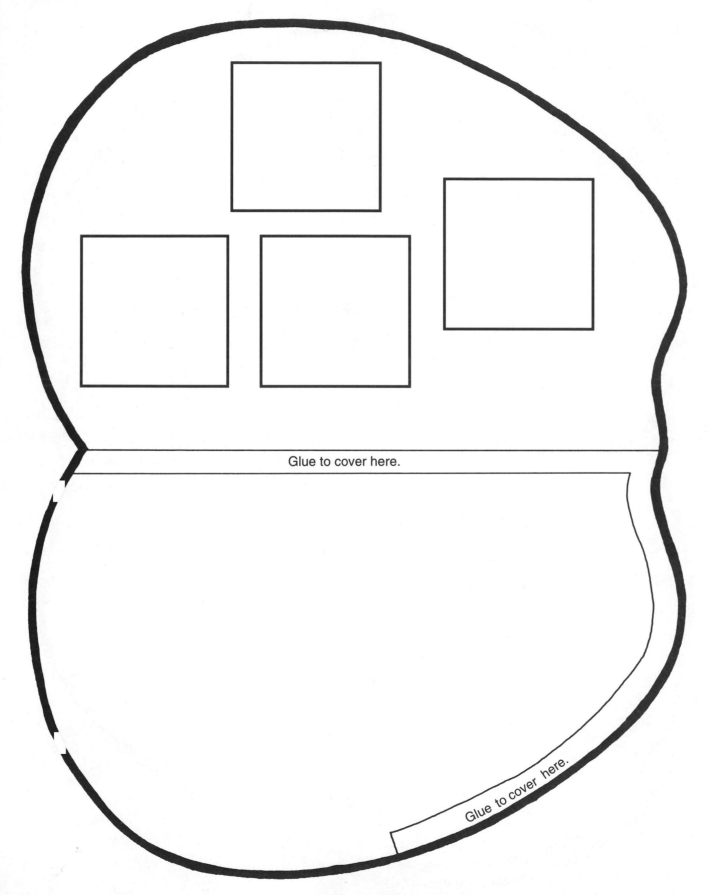

Glue to cover here.

Glue to cover here.

Use with the "Aa—Apple Cut-And-Paste Project" activity on page 5.

caterpillar

leaf

stem

picture cards

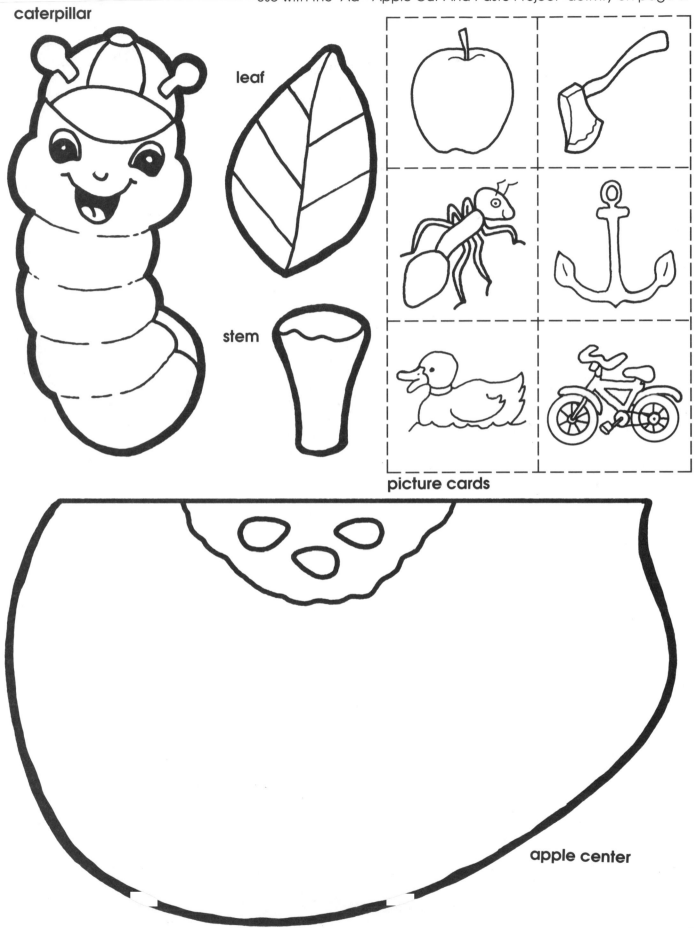

apple center

Pattern
Apple Tree Game
Use this with "The Apple Tree Game" activity on page 4.

A Is For Apple

A

a

Directions

1. Say the words.

2. Put the apples on the tree.

B is for bear

Teach your youngsters the "bear" facts about the letter B.

"Busy Bear" Action Poem

Have your youngsters perform the movement for each line.

Busy Bear, Busy Bear, turn around,
Busy Bear, Busy Bear, jump up and down.
Busy Bear, Busy Bear, walk to me,
Busy Bear, Busy Bear, bend your knee.
Busy Bear, Busy Bear, on your toes,
Busy Bear, Busy Bear, touch your nose.
Busy Bear, Busy Bear, hop around,
Busy Bear, Busy Bear, sit on the ground!

"B, b, Here Is A *B*"

Sing this bouncy B song to the tune of "Skip To My Lou."

B, b, here is a *B.*
B, b, here is a *B.*
B, b, here is a *B,*
Here is a *B* for me.

1. *B, b,* here is a book.
   B, b, here is a book.
   B, b, here is a book,
   Here is a book for me.

Additional verses:

2. *B, b,* here is a ball.
3. *B, b,* here is a bear.
4. *B, b,* here is a bed.
5. *B, b,* here is a bike.
6. *B, b,* here is a bird.

"Berry-licious" Biscuits

With the help of your youngsters, bake some biscuit bears to tempt their bear-sized appetites! Prepare a batch of your favorite drop biscuit dough. Have each student make a bear-shaped biscuit by dropping three spoonfuls of dough onto a prepared cookie sheet to resemble a bear's head and ears. Bake as directed in the recipe and allow the biscuits to cool. Carefully slice each bear biscuit with a serrated knife. Let each child choose from a selection of berry jams—inspired by the book *Jamberry* by Bruce Degen—to embellish his biscuit.

Bear-With-A-Bag Booklet Page

Use the *B* booklet page on page 13 as an independent story-starter activity, or have each child complete the page and save it to compile with the other pages into a book. Have each child trace and write the upper- and lowercase letter. Write each child's dictation to complete the sentence in the space provided. Cut and paste, or draw and color, *B* pictures in the bear's bag.

Big Bear Bag Puppet

Reproduce the bear face and paw patterns on page 14 on white construction paper. Let each child color her pattern pieces, adding eyes to the upper portion of the bear's head. Provide each child with a small, folded paper lunch bag. Cut out the upper portion of the head and glue it to the bag flap, aligning the straight edges. Cut out the lower portion of the head and glue it beneath the flap of the bag. Cut out the paws and glue them to the bag.

Bear With A Basket

Present your little ones with a basketful of letter *B* learning. Reproduce the patterns on pages 15, 16, and 17 on white construction paper. (To add additional possibilities for student work, mask the illustrations on the flap pieces. Let your students draw their own pictures to go with the words.) Cut out the bear and basket pattern piece. Cut out all six flap pieces. Stack the flap pieces with the "What's In Bear's Basket?" piece on top. Staple the flap pieces to the basket so that the straight edges of the flap pieces line up with the top edge of the basket, just below the bold upper- and lowercase *B*s.

Jamberry by Bruce Degen

- After reading the story, have your youngsters name all of the berries in the story. Have them point out the berries that begin with the letter *B*. Have them add to the list by naming other kinds of berries that do not start with *B* such as strawberry, gooseberry, and huckleberry.

- Let your youngsters be word detectives. Have them search the pages of the story for things that begin with *B*, other than berries. Make a list of these *B* words. Have each child illustrate a word on white drawing paper. Label each picture with its matching word.

- Discuss all the ways that we can prepare berries to eat. After listing all of the ideas, have each child select his favorite berry dish. Graph your students' selections to make a visual display of these berry special treats!

Best Bear Books

Bear Shadow by Frank Asch
Blackboard Bear by Martha Alexander
Blueberries For Sal by Robert McCloskey
Jesse Bear, What Will You Wear? by Nancy White Carlstrom
Little Bear by Else Holmelund Minarik

More Bear And *B* Activities

- Introduce the children to different berries that begin with the letter *B*. Fresh berries such as blueberries and blackberries can be found in the grocery store during certain times of the year. Spread a half slice of bread with blueberry, blackberry, or boysenberry jam for the students to taste.

- Have a Buddy Bear Day in your classroom and allow each child to bring in his favorite stuffed bear from home. Help the children choose categories to sort the bears into such as *bears with bows*, *bears with dresses*, *bears with pants*, or *bear colors*. Make a simple bar graph to record findings.

- Fill a box with empty food containers whose contents begin with *B*. List all the *B* foods the children have eaten each day.

- Supply the children with a large rubber ball and challenge them to <u>bounce</u> the <u>ball</u> as many times as they can in a row. Record the childrens' scores and give a bouncing-ball award.

- Ask the children to hypothesize which color gummy bear there is the most of in a package of gummy bears. Sort the package as a class and record how many of each color is found.

- Fill a small jar with different dried beans and encourage each student in the class to estimate how many beans are in the jar. Reinforce counting skills by allowing each child to count the beans and record the actual amount.

- Display a basket filled with books about bears. Choose children each day to pick out books to be read by the teacher.

B - - - - - - - - - - - - - - b - - - - - - - - - - - -

Bear

The bear has a bag.

Inside he has

Pattern
Bag Puppet
Use with the "Big Bear Bag Puppet" activity on page 11.

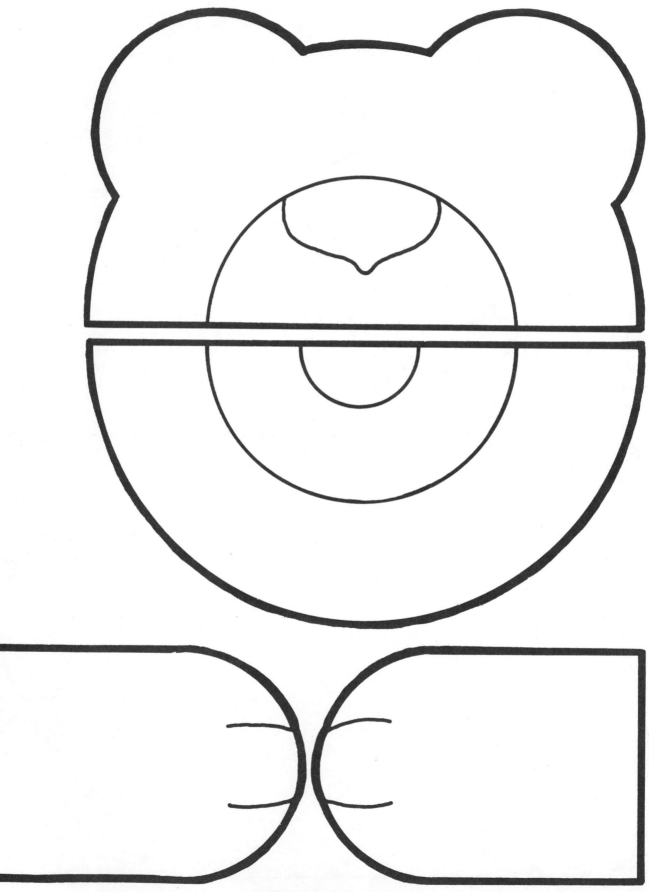

Bb

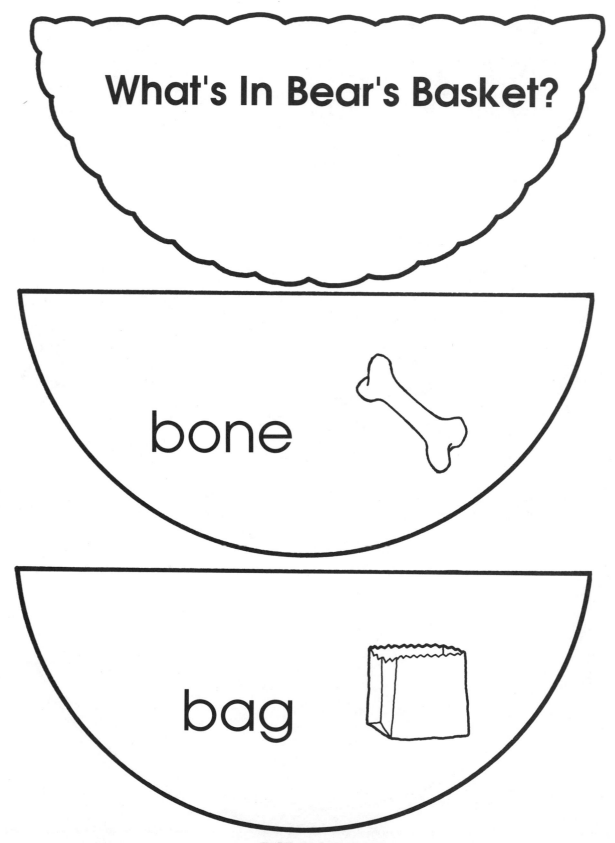

What's In Bear's Basket?

bone

bag

bell

book

C is for cat

Try these cute cat activities to delight your youngsters.

"Little Cat" Action Poem

This little cat has a funny hat.
[Point to head.]
This little cat spies a little bat.
[Look up and point up.]
This little cat smells a little rat!
[Make a sniffing noise.]

This little cat has a pretty cap.
[Point to head.]
This little cat sits upon my lap.
[Pretend to pet a cat.]
This little cat takes a little nap.
[Close eyes and pretend to sleep.]

Kitty Cat Sandwich

Preparing these cute sandwiches for a snack will be the cat's meow. Use a knife or cookie cutter to cut out a cat-shaped face from a slice of bread. Spread softened cream cheese on top of the cat's face. Let each child decorate his cat's face with two raisin eyes, a cheese triangle nose, and six thin celery slivers for whiskers.

"Carrie Had A Little Cat"

Here is "Mary Had A Little Lamb" with a feline twist.

1. Carrie had a little cat, little cat, little cat.
   Carrie had a little cat. Its fur was white as snow.

Additional verses:

2. Everywhere that Carrie went…the cat was sure to go.
3. It followed her to school one day. Oh, yes, the cat knew how.
4. It made the children laugh and play…to hear the cat meow.

Cat's Cap Booklet Page

Use the *C* booklet page on page 20 as previously directed for the letters *A* and *B.* Write each child's dictation to complete the sentence in the space provided. Have each child think of a name for the cat that begins with the letter *C.* Write this name on the bill of the cat's cap. Have each child color the cat and cap.

Celebrate C Cut-And-Paste

Let your youngsters light the candles on this little kitty's cake. Reproduce the large "Celebrate *C*" pattern on page 21 and the candle patterns on page 22 on white construction paper. Have your students color the "Celebrate *C*" page, cut out the candles and paste them to the cake.

To make a class game, reproduce page 21 on tagboard. Color, laminate, and cut out the gameboard. Reproduce the candles on page 22 on tagboard. Make two or three extra candles and program them with pictures that do not begin with *C.* Color, laminate, and cut out the candles. Have your students choose appropriate cards to put on the cake.

Cat In A Cap

Reproduce the pattern pieces on pages 23 and 24 on tagboard to make a sturdy manipulative activity for each of your youngsters. Have each child color her cat and cap, adding eyes, a nose, and whiskers to the cat's face. Then cut out the shape. Each child can also color, cut out, and glue the block letter *C* between the cat's paws. Carefully cut out the triangular space on the cap along the dotted lines. For young students, attach the picture wheel to the cap with a brad at the circles. For older students, attach the word wheel. Let each older student add a word to her wheel in the space provided.

Have You Seen My Cat? by Eric Carle

* Look at the pictures of the cats in the book. Ask your youngsters if they can name each type of wild cat; then check the endpaper illustrations for the correct names. Have your students tell you what characteristics make all of these cats similar. Label a bulletin board with the words "Cats, Cats, Cats." Ask students to paint pictures of different cats, both wild and domestic. Post the cat paintings on the bulletin board.

* Have your youngsters describe what each cat in the book is doing; then give them the opportunity to act like cats. Have students pretend to walk, run, snarl, meow, and sleep like the cats in the story.

* Ask each student to create a crayon drawing of an imaginary pet cat. Have him make up a name for the cat that begins with the letter *C*. Have each student complete the sentence below with a verb that begins with *C* as well:
  "My cat [name that begins with *C*] likes to [verb that begins with *C*]."

Other Cat Tales

The Cat In The Hat by Dr. Seuss
The Farmyard Cat by Christine Anello
Here Comes The Cat! by Vladimir Vagin and Frank Asch
Millions Of Cats by Wanda Gag
Puss In Boots by Charles Perrault

More Cat and *C* Activities

* Have a Cap Day celebration and allow the students to wear a cap to school. Use the parent note on page 22 to notify parents.

* Slice prepackaged, rolled cookie dough into enough thin slices for each student to a have slice. Show students how to pinch the top to make ears and add red hots for eyes, nose, and mouth. Use black string licorice for whiskers if desired. Bake as directed on package.

* Explain to students that cats do not need to take a bath. Discuss how cats and other animals such as lions and tigers bathe themselves. Tell the students that although mother cat licks her babies to clean them, this is an instinctive trait and they do not learn it from mother. All cats automatically know how to do this.

* Make your snack a *C* treat by serving cocoa and crackers. Help the students think of other *C* foods and list them on large bulletin board paper *C*.

* Pass out a chocolate-chip cookie to each student and ask him how he can find out how many chocolate chips are in his cookie. Take all suggestions and then allow the children to "mine" their cookies and count the chips. Record the findings on a large, paper chocolate-chip cookie.

* Bring in a canned food and introduce the children to the cylinder shape of the can. Have the children name other cylinder-shaped objects. Store a large coffee can in your room and encourage students to bring items that begin with *C* to put inside.

Cat

Cat has a colorful cap.

She wears it

Celebrate C

Patterns
Candles
Use with the "Celebrate *C* Cut-And-Paste" activity on page 18.

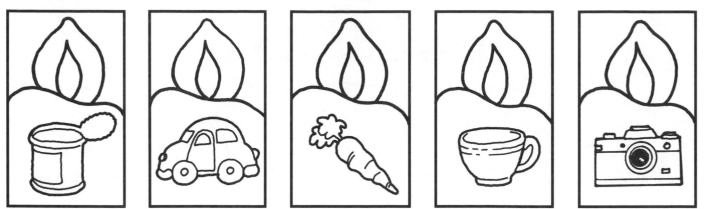

Parent Note
Use with the "More Cat and *C* Activities" on page 19.

Dear Parent,

Our class is learning about the letter **C**.
We will have Cap Day on

_____.

Please send a baseball-style cap to school with your child on that day.

Thanks!

Cut
this
out.

O

Patterns

Use with the "Cat In A Cap" activity on page 19.

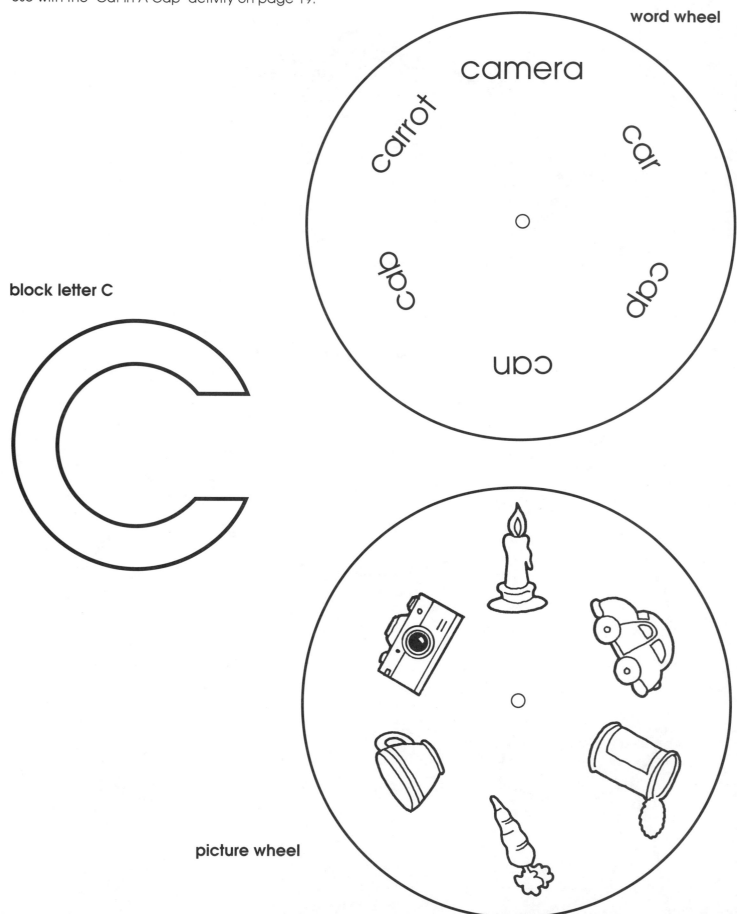

block letter C

picture wheel

©The Education Center, Inc. • TEC251

D  is for dinosaur

Dare to teach *D* with darling dinosaurs.

"Five Funny Dinosaurs" Counting Poem

Practice counting with this poem.

Five funny dinosaurs
Standing by a door.
One walked out and
Then there were four.

Four funny dinosaurs
Standing by the sea.
One jumped in
Then there were three.

Three funny dinosaurs
Standing in the zoo.
One ran away and
Then there were two.

Two funny dinosaurs
Standing in the sun.
One went inside and
Then there was one.

One funny dinosaur
Standing all alone.
He walked away and
Then there were none!

Dinosaur Dessert

Spread dinosaur graham cookies with one of the following delicious fillings to make a dreamy sandwich:

- cream cheese spread mixed with honey
- cream cheese mixed with diced dried apricots or apricot jam
- peanut butter and chopped banana
- peanut butter and raisins
- cheddar cheese spread mixed with chopped apple
- cheddar cheese spread and shelled, salted sunflower seeds

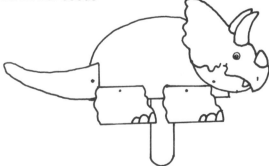

"Di-no-saurs!"

This "dino-lightful" song is sung to the tune of "Three Blind Mice."

Di-no-saurs! Di-no-saurs!
Lived long ago. Lived long ago.
Some were as little as chickens, you see.
Some were so very much bigger than me.
Oh, wouldn't you like to be able to see
A di-no-saur!

Happy Dinosaur Booklet Page

Use the *D* booklet page on page 27 as directed for previous letters. Write each child's dictation to complete the sentence in the space provided on the dinosaur. Have each child color the dinosaur's head, tail, and legs.

Dinosaur Stick Puppet

Use the patterns on page 28 to make an articulated stick puppet. Reproduce the page on tagboard for sturdiness. Color each shape with crayons or sponge-print each shape with thinned tempera paint. Let dry and then cut out. Glue the center of the body to a craft stick or tongue depressor. Attach the head, legs, and tail to the body with brads.

"What Can Dinosaurs Do?" Book

Help your youngsters put together this dandy little *D* book quicker than you can say, "Di-no-saur!" Each page of the book features a different dinosaur displaying a different *D* action word. Have your youngsters complete the pages with their own words and artwork to make the book extra special. Reproduce the six book sections on pages 29, 30, and 31 on white construction paper. Cut the sections apart. Help each student complete the sections as directed, stack them in sequence, and staple together.

Cover Color the dinosaur. Write name on the byline.
Page 1 Write in a song title to complete the sentence.
Page 2 Draw something in the frame. Complete the sentence.
Page 3 Draw something in the hole. Complete the sentence.
Page 4 Draw something on the table. Complete the sentence.
Page 5 Draw something on the paper. Complete the sentence.

Big Old Bones by Carol Carrick

- Professor Potts and his wife put together a very big, though very strange, dinosaur. Help your youngsters decorate a large dinosaur of their own. Enlarge one of the dinosaurs from the "What Can Dinosaurs Do?" book (pages 29–31). Make a very large outline on bulletin-board paper. Prepare sponge-printers in the shape of the letter *D*. Use tempera paint in a variety of colors to print the letter *D* all over the dino's body.

- Reproduce the stick puppet patterns on page 28 on two colors of tagboard. Write uppercase *D*s on each piece of the dinosaur of one color. Write lowercase *d*s on each piece of the other color. Cut out all of the pieces and mix them up. Have your youngsters sort the pieces by color and by letter.

Additional Dinosaur Books

Bones, Bones, Dinosaur Bones by Byron Barton
Dinosaur Dream by Dennis Nolan
The Dinosaur Who Lived In My Backyard by
  B. G. Hennessy
How I Captured A Dinosaur by Henry Schwartz
Prehistoric Pinkerton by Steven Kellogg
The Tyrannosaurus Game by Steven Kroll

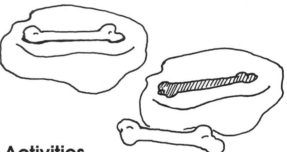

More Dinosaur and *D* Activities

- Tell the children that no human has ever seen a real dinosaur but that we know they once lived on earth because we find their bones and fossils. Make a fossil with the students by pressing a chicken bone into clay. Allow the children to make prints of other items that might be found many years from now such as dice, diaper pins, or dimes.

- Plan a dinosaur day and have each student bring in a favorite dinosaur toy, model, or book.

- Help the children try to estimate the size of a dinosaur. Premeasure a piece of string to 100 feet and wind it around a piece of cardboard so it is easily unwound. Take the class outside and ask a student to hold one end of the string. Then ask the students, if the dinosaur's nose was at the end of the string, where do you think the tip of his tail would be? Allow the children to stand at the place they choose. Unwind the string while walking. When the string is completely unwound, explain to the children that some dinosaurs were 100 feet long.

- Plan a class dinosaur meal and list any silly ingredients that begin with the letter *D*. Mix up a delicious dino drink of green Kool-Aid for the children to sample with little dinosaur-shaped crackers or cookies.

- Have the children imagine how a dinosaur might dance. Allow the children to dino dance to music.

Dinosaur

The dinosaur is happy.

It is happy because

Patterns

Use with the "Dinosaur Stick Puppet" activity on page 25 and the *Big Old Bones* activity on page 26.

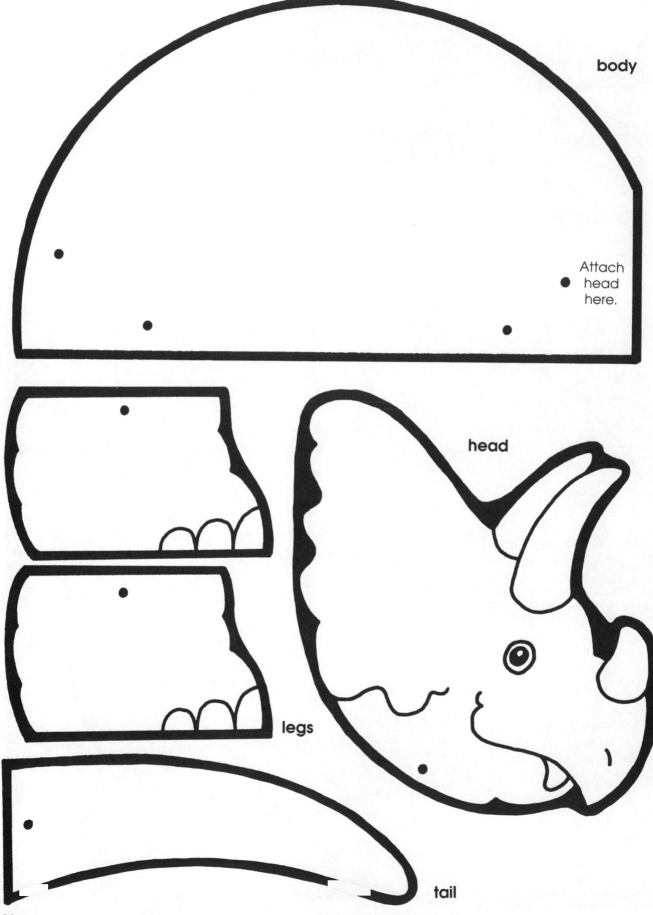

body

Attach
head
here.

head

legs

tail

What Can Dinosaurs Do?

Dd

by _____

Dinosaurs can dance.

This dinosaur's favorite song is

1

Dinosaurs can decorate.

This dinosaur made a picture of

2

Dinosaurs can dig.

This dinosaur dug up a

3

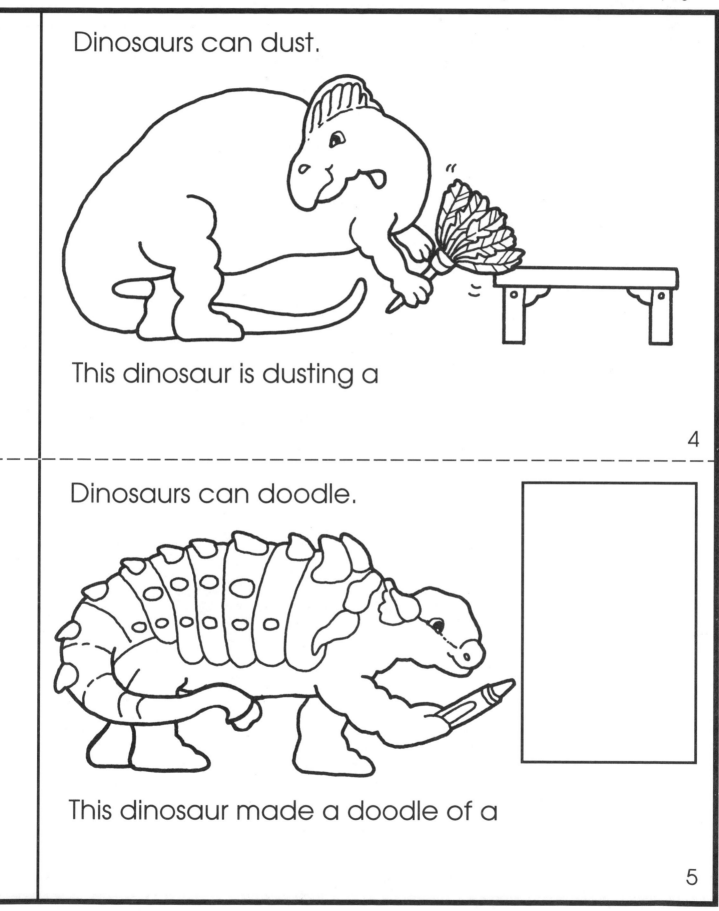

Dinosaurs can dust.

This dinosaur is dusting a

4

Dinosaurs can doodle.

This dinosaur made a doodle of a

5

E is for elephant

These elephant activities will inspire eager learners.

"One Little Elephant"
Practice counting with this poem.

No little elephants.
What can be done?
I see an elephant.
That makes one.

One little elephant
At the zoo.
Add another elephant.
That makes two.

Two little elephants
By the sea.
Add another elephant.
That makes three.

Three little elephants
On the floor.
Add another elephant.
That makes four.

Four little elephants
That I see.
Hope they'll come and
Play with me!

Elephant Eats
Assemble an elephant that your youngsters will really enjoy! Provide each child with a small napkin or plate and the following ingredients:
Head—One mini rice cake spread with peanut butter.
Ears—Two apple slices.
Eyes—Two raisins or two peanut halves.
Trunk—A carrot strip or carrot curl or a small section of fruit roll-up.

"The Elephant Song"
This is sung to the tune of "The Farmer In The Dell."

1. The elephant swings his trunk. *(Use arms to make a*
    The elephant swings his trunk. *swinging trunk motion.)*
    High-ho the derry-o;
    The elephant swings his trunk.

Additional verses:

2. The elephant flaps his ears.
    (Use hands to make flapping ears.)
3. The elephant stomps his feet.
    (Stomp feet.)
4. The elephant swings his tail.
    (Swing backside back and forth.)

Elephant Booklet Page
Use the *E* booklet page on page 34 as directed for previous letters. Write each child's dictation to describe what he thinks the elephant likes to do. Then have him color the elephant.

Elegant Elephants
Help your youngsters create elephants with lovely "wrinkled" skin. Reproduce the ear and trunk patterns on page 36 and the body pattern on page 35 on heavy white paper. Reproduce one set for each child. Have each youngster press firmly to color the three elephant body parts with gray crayon. Lightly brush the crayoned work with a very thin, black tempera-paint wash. Do not "scrub" the brush over the crayon. The heavy crayon will resist the paint, but the paint will soak into the uncrayoned areas. When the elephant pieces are dry, cut them out. Glue the trunk and ear to the head area, as indicated. Let each child glue on a length of twine, rickrack, or yarn for a tail and a construction-paper eye. Post the pachyderms on a bulletin board titled "Elegant Elephants."

Elephant Foldout Book

Reproduce the patterns on pages 36, 37, and 38 on white construction paper. Have your youngsters color the two elephant pieces (page 37) and cut them out. Have them cut out the two book page strips (page 38) and then glue all four of the cut-out pieces together as indicated. Color the *E* picture pieces (page 36), cut them out, and glue them to the matching sections in the book. Fold up the book accordion-style and fold out to read.

The Right Number Of Elephants
by Jeff Sheppard

- The elephants in this story have lots of energy! Have your youngsters describe the energetic actions of the elephants on each page. Ask them to imagine how the child in the story came to have so many elephants in his neighborhood.

- Write short sentences describing classroom tasks and activities on sentence strips. Place the strips in a box and have each child take out a strip. Read the task or activity to the child and have her describe how many elephants it would take to perform each one.

- Reproduce the elephant illustration from the elephant booklet page on page 34 on gray construction paper so that you have ten elephants. Cut out the elephants and post them on a bulletin board or wall at the children's eye level. Trace the numerals one through ten on colored construction paper and cut them out. Have your youngsters glue the cut-out numerals to the elephants' backs to create a number line.

Additional Elephant Adventures

Alexander's Midnight Snack: A Little Elephant's ABC by Catherine Stock
Babar books by Jean and Laurent de Brunhoff
Ella The Bad Speller by Robert Kraus
Engelbert The Elephant by Tom Paxton
Frank And Ernest by Alexandra Day

More Elephant and *E* Activities

- Bring in a item made from ivory and explain to your students that it came from an elephant's tusk. The tusks are actually the elephant's teeth and hunters are no longer allowed to hunt elephants for the ivory.

- Display a large basket filled with small plastic eggs in the room. Have the students brainstorm words that begin with *E* and write them on a piece of paper. Put each idea into an egg. Allow a child to choose an *E* egg each day and use the word inside as your *E* password for the day.

- Take a short field trip around your school to find all the Es in the exit signs. Have the children explain why they think the signs are written in red. Make EXIT signs for your classroom door.

- Provide each child with a large envelope. Have him cut out the letter *E* from magazine or newspaper ads and glue them to the *E* envelope.

- Have an *E* Egg Day and provide egg-salad sandwiches, hard-boiled eggs, or candy eggs for an "eggs-citing" snack.

Elephant

This elephant has energy. She likes to

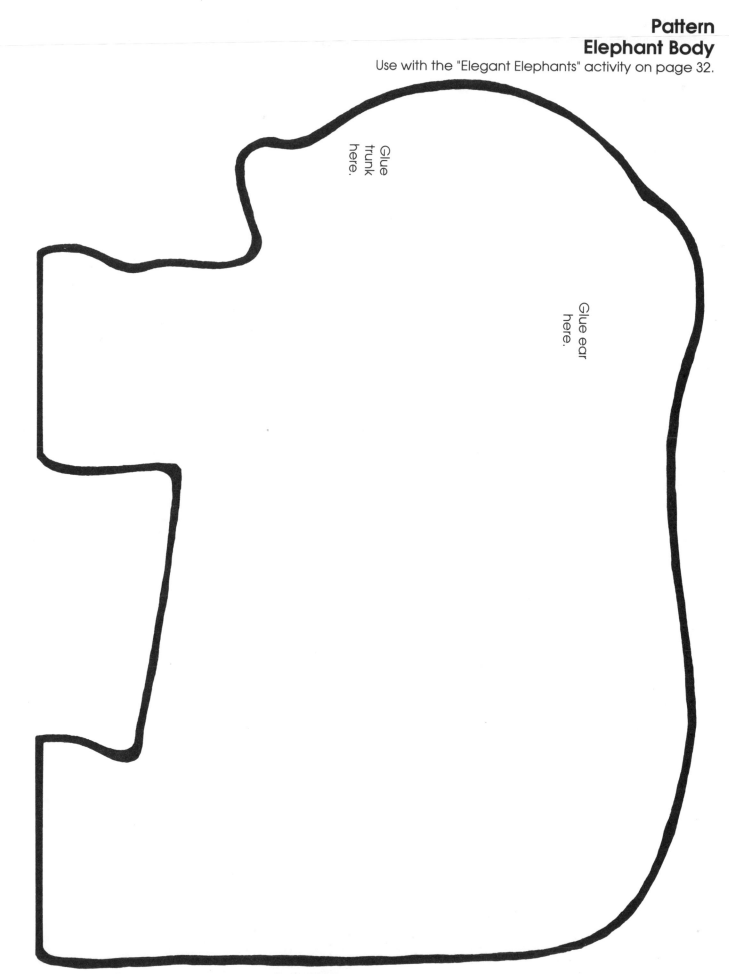

Glue
trunk
here.

Glue ear
here.

Patterns
Elephant Ear And Trunk
Use with the "Elegant Elephants" activity on page 32.

trunk

ear

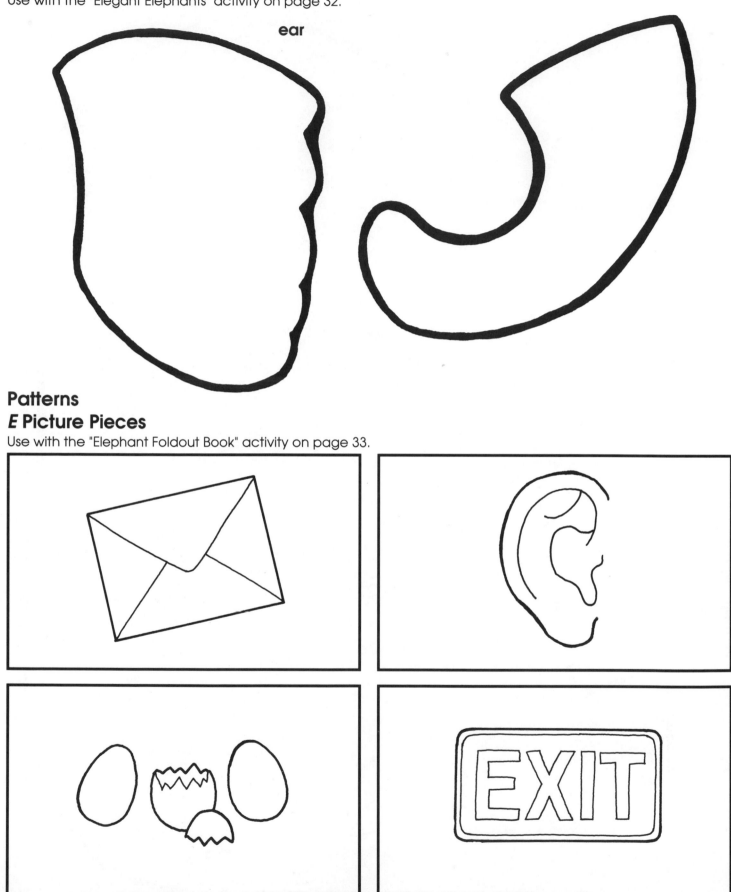

Patterns
E Picture Pieces
Use with the "Elephant Foldout Book" activity on page 33.

©The Education Center, Inc. • TEC251

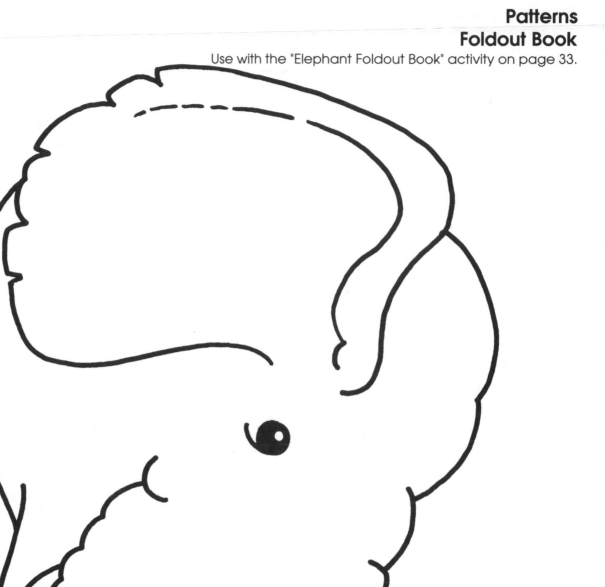

face

trunk

Foldout Book Page Patterns

Use with the "Elephant Foldout Book" activity on page 33.

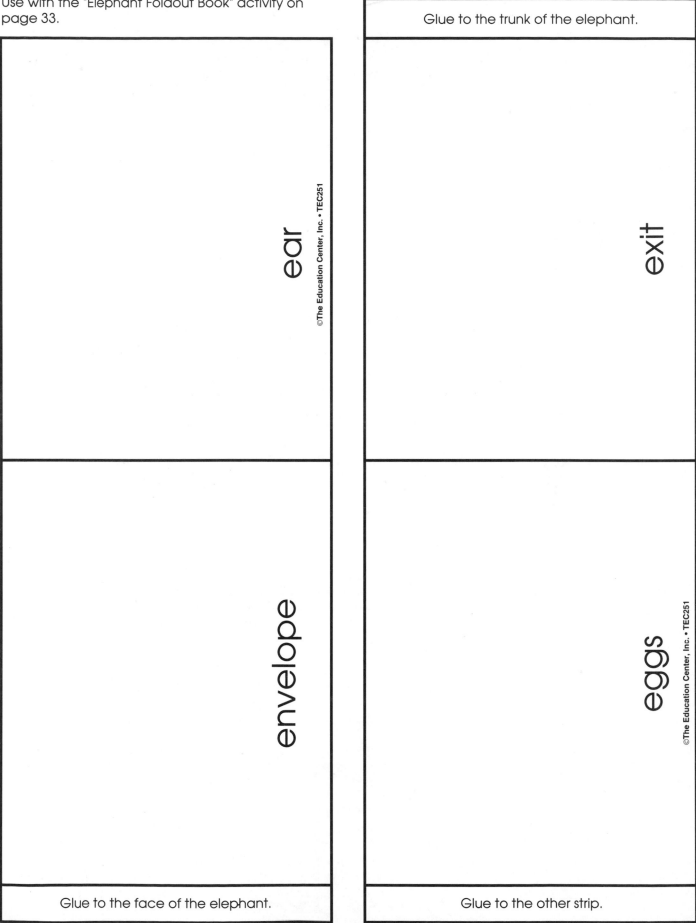

Glue to the trunk of the elephant.

ear

exit

©The Education Center, Inc. • TEC251

envelope

eggs

©The Education Center, Inc. • TEC251

Glue to the face of the elephant.

Glue to the other strip.

F is for fish

Inspire something "fishy" with these *F* activities.

"Four Little Fish"

Challenge your little ones to come up with their own swimming and directional motions to accompany the poem.

1. Swish, swish, swish.
   See four little fish.
   See four little fish in the sea.
   Swim up and down, swim all around.
   Swish, little fish, in the sea.

Repeat the verse, substituting a new line for line four each time.

2. Swim in and out; swim all about.
3. Swim fast and slow; swim as you go.
4. Swim low and high; now say good-bye!

Fishy Food For All

Fix a few snacks with a decidedly marine theme. First cut fish shapes from slices of whole wheat bread. Top each whole wheat fish with tuna salad; then embellish with a slice of pimento-filled green olive for an eye.

For a second course, spread peanut butter on celery pieces. Top each piece with four goldfish crackers.

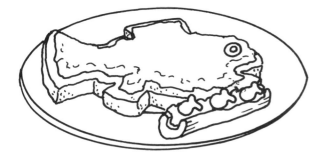

"Did You Ever See A Fishy?"

"Did You Ever See A Lassie?" meets the deep blue sea in this simple song.

1. Did you ever see a fishy, a fishy, a fishy?
   Did you ever see a fishy, swim this way and that?
   Swim this way and that way, and that way and this way.
   Did you ever see a fishy, swim this way and that?

2. Swish this way and that.
3. Splash this way and that.
4. Splish this way and that.

Fish Booklet Page

Use the *F* booklet page on page 41 as directed for previous letters. Write each child's dictation to complete the sentence to tell what the fish found. Have each youngster draw a picture of the fish's catch in the space below the fish.

Fishbowl

Present your youngsters with the perfect pets: fish in a fishbowl that never needs cleaning! Reproduce the patterns on pages 43, 44, and 45 on white construction paper. Have your youngsters color the two fishbowl pages, then cut them out on the bold lines. Carefully cut the castle doorway along the dotted lines. Have your students color the three little fish on page 45, cut them out, and glue them to the castle fishbowl, leaving the doorway unblocked. Staple the two pages together with the "*F* is for Fish" page on top. Help students glue the two sections of the picture strip together, then thread the strip through the castle doorway. To use, pull the strip to reveal each picture in the doorway.

Fish In A Fingerpaint Sea

Your youngsters can float some fancy fish in their own fingerpaint sea. Ask each child to create a large, finger-painted picture of the ocean using blue and/or green fingerpaint. Provide each youngster with a copy of the fish patterns on page 42, which has been duplicated on white construction paper. Have each child color the fish and add details with paint, then cut out the fish and glue them to the dry finger painting. Embellish the marine scene further with copies of the letter *F* cut from colored construction paper.

Swimmy by Leo Lionni

- Read this fun story and delight your youngsters with the surprisingly fishy ending. Prepare a sheet of bulletin-board paper with a large fish outline. Pencil in the outline with a light hand so that your youngsters can't obviously see it. Cut fish-shaped sponge printers using the Swimmy-shaped pattern at the top of page 42. Print one shape on the paper with black paint to represent the eye. Direct students in printing more fish shapes with red paint within the outline to make one big fish.

- Look at the pictures in the book and have students find all of the true fish. Point out that an eel *is* a fish, a jellyfish *is not* really a fish, and seaweed is a plant.

- Have each youngster write a sentence or two to describe one of the fish in the book. Title each child's story "Swimmy's Fishy Friend" and have each child create a crayon illustration to accompany her fish tale.

Fabulous Fish Tales

Big Al by Andrew Clements
Fish Eyes: A Book You Can Count On by Lois Ehlert
Fishing Is For Me by Art Thomas
The Magic Fish by Freya Littledale
The Rainbow Fish by Marcus Pfister

More Fish And *F* Activities

- Explain to the children that fish have gills that allow them to take air out of water. Hold up a clear glass of water and ask if they can see the air in the water. Allow the glass to sit for several hours and the children will begin to observe bubbles on the inside of the glass.

- After reviewing the fact that fish must live in water, tell the students you are going to have some fun with words. Give them the following example: *If fish had feet, they could walk to school.* Have several students finish the sentence in different ways. If fish had feet, _____. Try others such as *if fish had fingers*, *if fish had French fries*, or *if fish had fingerpaint.*

- Teach your youngsters to play Go Fish with playing cards.

- Cut a large blue construction-paper fish bowl for each student and give them four gummy fish each; three to glue to the bowl and one to eat. Have the students draw plants, gravel, and rocks with crayons.

- Organize a Find It hunt in your room. Hide the following items in your room: one flag, two fake fish (toys or pictures), three furry friends (stuffed animals), four feathers, and five forks. Reward each searcher with a fig-bar cookie.

- Fill a small fish bowl with goldfish crackers and have the children use them for counting practice or as counters for addition problems. They get to eat their counters when the work is complete.

Fish

What a fancy fish!

The fish found a

Patterns
Fish
Use with the "Fish In A Fingerpaint Sea" and *Swimmy* activities on page 40.

42

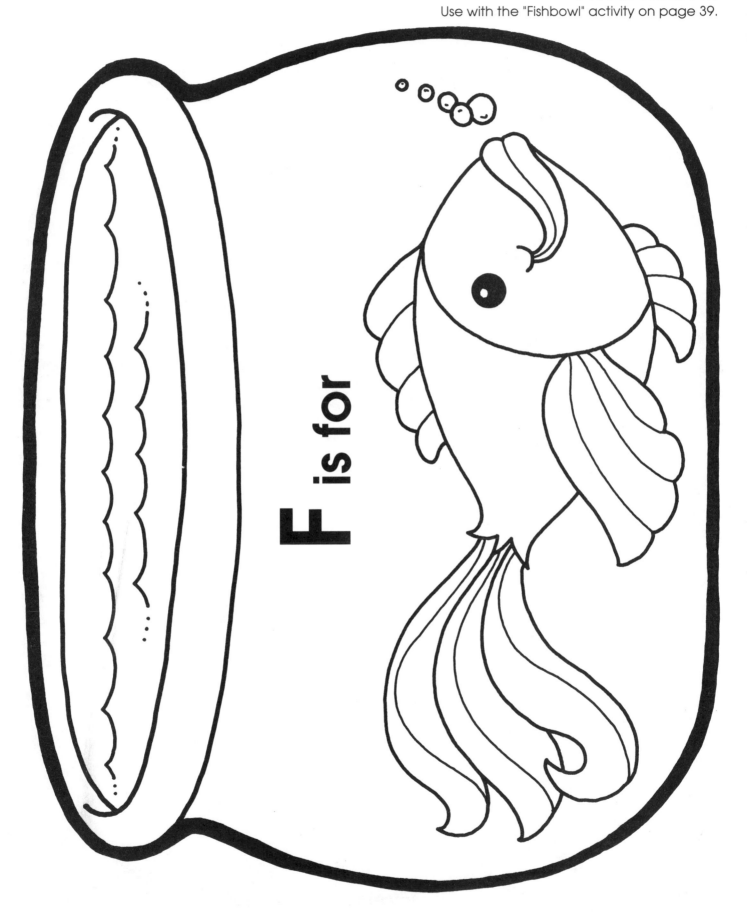

F **is for**

Pattern
Castle
Use with the "Fishbowl" activity on page 39.

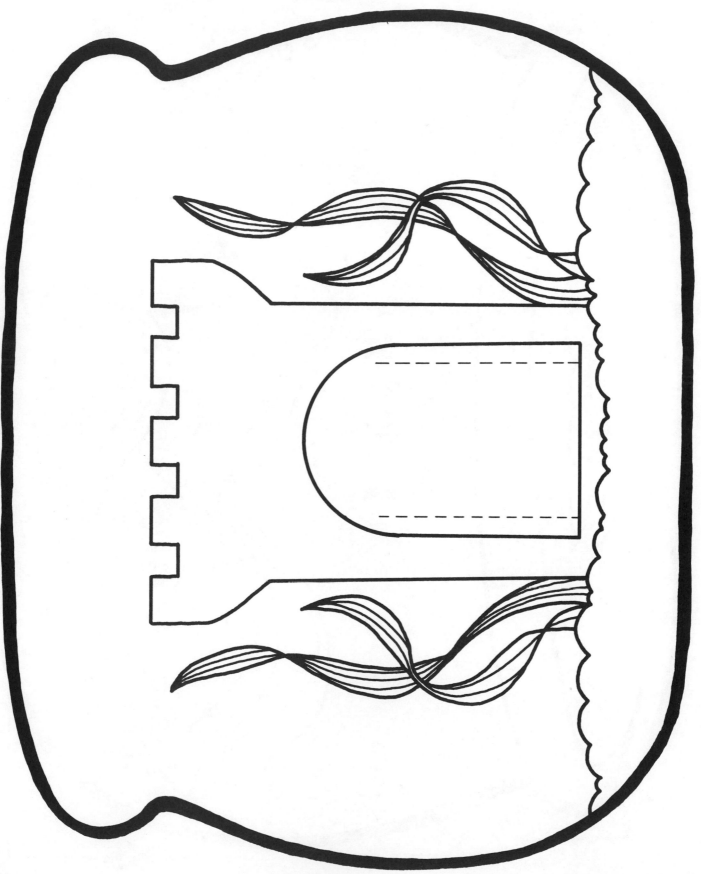

little fish

picture strip

picture strip

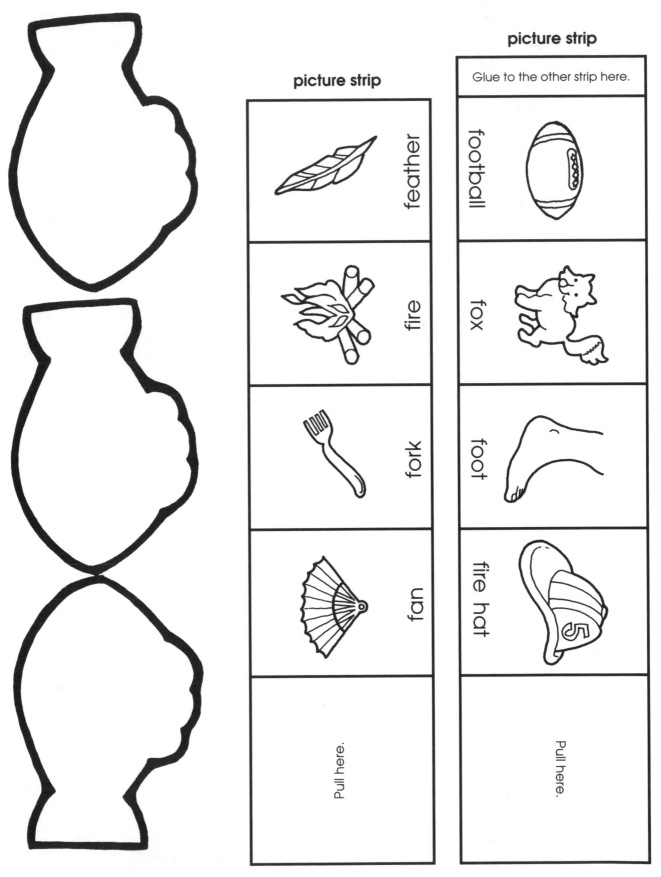

G is for goat

Goats galore will encourage your kids to learn about *G*.

"Once I Had A Little Goat"

Your little kids can pretend to be little goats as they recite each version of the poem, one for your girls and one for your boys.

1.   Once I had a little goat.
      Her eyes were very brown.
      I dressed her in a [flowered hat]
      And took her into town.

2. & 3. *Repeat the verse two more times. Replace the dress-up item in line three with [pretty bow] and [ruffled skirt].*

      End with the following verse:

4.   Once I had a little goat.
      Her eyes were very brown.
      I dressed her up so she would be
      The fairest goat in town!

5., 6., 7. *Repeat the poem for your boys. Use the following dress-up items: [funny hat], [nice bow tie], [checkered vest]*

      End with the following verse:

8.   Once I had a little goat.
      His eyes were very brown.
      I dressed him up so he would be
      The finest goat in town!

Great Grass Goodies

Give your youngsters these great goodies to graze on at snacktime. Top your little kids' favorite crackers with cream cheese spread or cheddar cheese spread. Sprinkle a little alfalfa sprout "grass" atop each cheese-spread cracker. Serve these treats with small cups of "grass juice": milk tinted with a small amount of green food coloring.

"Climb, Climb, Little Goats"

This is sung to the tune of "Row, Row, Row Your Boat."

      Climb, climb, little goats.
      Climb up on the hill.
      Up and up and up and up.
      Goats up on the hill.

Add a different verb such as *leap, hop, walk,* or *dance* each time you sing the song. Add movements, if desired.

Goat In The Garden Booklet Page

Use the *G* booklet page on page 48 as directed for previous letters. Have your youngsters draw flowers and vegetables within the open-space garden or cut pictures from garden catalogs to glue within the space. Write each child's dictation within the space provided above and to the left of the goat.

Goat's Garden Game

Make a great game with the patterns on pages 49 and 50. Reproduce the Goat's Garden gameboard on tagboard or white construction paper, color, and laminate for durability. Reproduce the grass cards on tagboard or light green construction paper, laminate, and cut out. To play the game, have a student choose a grass card, say the name of the picture, and place it on the garden gameboard. To add difficulty, make additional grass cards which you have programmed with pictures that begin with *D* or *J*.

Inside Goat's Garage

This little goat's garage is full of things that begin with *G!* To make the project, reproduce the Goat's garage pattern on page 51 on tagboard. Let your youngsters color the illustration and then cut the piece out on the bold outline. Reproduce the picture pages on pages 51 and 52 on white construction paper. Cut the picture pages apart and stack them, placing the "Things That Begin With *G"* title page on top. Center the stacked pages in the garage opening and staple them to the garage where indicated.

The Three Billy Goats Gruff
by Janet Stevens

- Have your youngsters study each billy goat's getup. Have them tell you how the goats used the costumes to fool the troll. Have each child tell you what he would wear to look small and what he would wear to look big and strong.

- Ask each youngster to choose one of the three goats to write about. Brainstorm a list of boys' and girls' names that begin with *G.* Have students select a *G*-name from the list for their goat. Have them use their selections to complete the following story sentences:

  "My name is [*G*-name].
  I am the [littlest/middle-sized/biggest] Billy Goat Gruff.
  I am very [descriptive phrase]."

- Enlarge and reproduce the goat illustration on the Goat's Garden gameboard on page 49 to make goats in three sizes. Color each goat and cut it out. Use these goats as flannelboard figures or as stick puppets to accompany an oral retelling of the story.

Good *G* Reads

Get That Goat! by Michael Aushenker (edited by Nancy R. Thatch)
The Goat In The Rug by Charles L. Blood and Martin Link
Gregory, The Terrible Eater by Mitchell Sharmat
Hattie The Goat by Abigail Pizer
Nanny Goat's Boat by Jane Belk Moncure

More Goat and *G* Activities

- Explain to your students that we have more than one word to describe many things. Refer back to the word *gruff* in the story *The Three Billy Goats Gruff.* Ask them what gruff means and if they can think of any other words that mean the same thing such as grouchy or grumpy. Have the students name a character that is gruff or grumpy.

- Glue pictures of garden plants cut from a gardening catalog to a large paper *G.* Help the students name the plants and circle any plant pictures that begin with *G.*

- Plant a wildflower garden in your classroom. Line a dress box with foil, add potting soil, and sow a packet of wildflower seeds. Keep the soil moist.

- Make a garbage collage. Glue assorted clean castoffs such as paper, small plastic items, bottle caps, and aluminum foil to Styrofoam meat trays. Hang the completed collages on a bulletin board titled "Glorious Garbage."

- Place mini plastic garbage cans around your room to hold pencils, crayons, scissors, and other school supplies.

- Serve gorp (Good Old Raisins & Peanuts) for a goat snack.

- Award each youngster the "Rated G" badge on page 50.

G   g

Goat

A goat went into the garden.

In the garden grew

Use with the "Goat's Garden Game" activity on page 46.
Use the goat from *The Three Billy Goats Gruff* on page 47.

Goat's Garden

Patterns

Use with the "Goat's Garden Game" activity on page 46.

grass cards

Pattern
Badge

Use with the last "More Goat and G Activities" on page 47.

This Kid is rated **G** for **Great!**

Pattern
Goat's garage
Use with the "Inside Goat's Garage" activity on page 47.

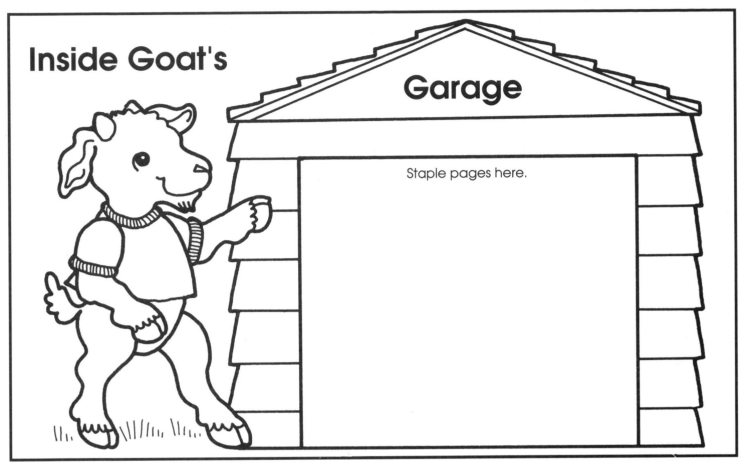

Inside Goat's Garage

Staple pages here.

Patterns
Picture Pages
Use with the "Inside Goat's Garage" activity on page 47.
These picture pages continue on page 52.

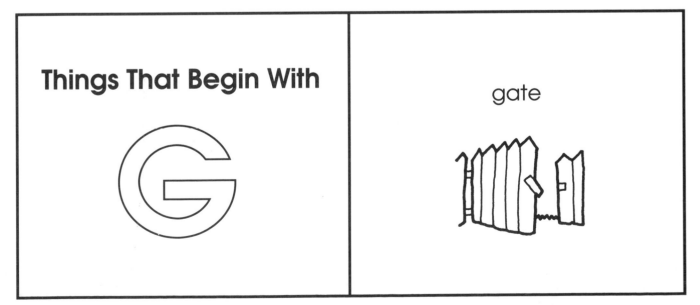

Things That Begin With G

gate

Patterns
Picture Pages
Use with the "Inside Goat's Garage" activity on page 47.

gas

garbage

game

girl

guitar

gum

H is for hat

Cover a hat full of *H* activities.

"Little Hat" Action Poem

Have your youngsters perform a new action each time they recite the poem.

> I had a funny little hat.
> My little hat was red.
> My hat could make me [fly around]
> When it was on my head!

Replace the action words in line three with *jump around, hop around, dance around,* etc.

Handsome Muffin Hats

Turn a conventional muffin on its head and you'll create a great snack chapeau!

Choose any favorite muffin recipe or packaged mix, and bake small muffins in prepared muffin tins. Do not use paper baking cups. Cool baked muffins. Place each child's muffin upside down on a napkin or plate. Decorate the muffin hats with small flower-shaped cookie sprinkles. Use a dab of tube frosting or frosting gel to attach each flower to the muffin.

"Put Your Hat On Your Head"

Sing this action song to the tune of "If You're Happy And You Know It."

1. Put your hat on your [head], on your [head].
   Put your hat on your head, on your head.
   Can you do what I said? Put your hat on your head.
   Put your hat on your head, on your head!

2. Put your hat on your [toes]; Can you do what I suppose?
3. Put your hat on your [knee]; Can you do it, one, two, three?
4. Put your hat on your [face]; Can you put it right in place?

Hat Booklet Page

Use the *H* booklet page on page 55 as directed for previous letters. Have children decorate the hat with flower pictures cut from magazines, paper doily scraps, and small fabric scraps. Write each child's dictation describing his hat in the space provided.

Create A Hat

Let your youngsters design a fanciful hat using the patterns on pages 56 and 57. Reproduce the patterns for the hat decorations on white construction paper. Provide one sheet for each child to color and embellish with glitter or dimensional paint. Provide a copy of the large *H* pattern on page 59 for children to add to their hats. Use the half-hat pattern on page 56 to make a full-sized tagboard tracer. Trace a hat shape on white construction paper for each child. Draw a line across the hat to define the brim. Have each student cut out her hat and her hat decorations and glue the decorations as desired above the hat brim line. Let each child decide who this fanciful hat might be for. Write each child's ideas on her hat within the space provided.

Hat Tachistoscope

Nothing can top this hat tachistoscope project for hands-on learning fun. Reproduce the hat, picture strips, and hat word card patterns on pages 58 and 59 on white construction paper. Color and cut them out. Cut along the dotted lines with an X-acto knife. Cut out the two picture strips and glue them together, then thread the strip through the flower. Cut out the hat word card and glue it to the hat brim. Pull the strip to reveal each picture.

Jennie's Hat by Ezra Jack Keats

- After reading the story, have your youngsters discuss the things that Jennie used as make-believe hats. Have them generate a list of things in the classroom that they could try on as pretend toppers. Let each student have a chance to actually try these on and then take a few photographs for fun!

- Ask your youngsters to speculate on why the ladies in the story were wearing such fancy hats. Have them compare these hats to hats that girls and women might wear today. Ask your students to discuss the kinds of hats that they might wear for various events and activities.

- With the help of some friendly birds, Jennie's hat was transformed. Provide each youngster with a classic folded newspaper hat and lots of glue, construction paper, colorful magazine pictures, and fabric scraps. Encourage them to pull out all the stops and decorate like mad!

Top Hat Tales

Aunt Flossie's Hats (And Crab Cakes Later) by Elizabeth Fitzgerald Howard
Away Went The Farmer's Hat by Jane Belk Moncure
The Garden Party by Margaret Mahy
Hats, Hats, Hats by Ann Morris

More Hat and *H* Activities

- Display a large hat filled with *H* items in your classroom. Have each child choose an item and tell its name.

- Collect several hats associated with different careers and test your students' knowledge. Have students try on hats and tell about their jobs.

- Bring in hats from different parts of the United States, ethnic backgrounds, and countries. Help your students identify the origin.

- Judge a hopping contest. Have your students stand up and hop on one foot. They continue hopping until they lose their balance and have to put the other foot down. At that time, they must sit down. The last student left hopping is the winner.

- Show a picture of a home and ask if every animal lives in the same kind of home. Explain that this particular home belongs to humans. Display pictures of homes of different animals and have the students identify the inhabitants.

- Use a cookie cutter to cut heart shapes out of bread. For a double *H* snack, bring in honey in a squeeze bottle and allow each child to make an *H* on his bread heart.

Hat

Here is my hat. I decorated it with

Pattern
Half Hat
Use with the "Create A Hat" activity on page 53.

Place on fold.

Pattern

Use with the "Hat Tachistoscope" activity on page 54.

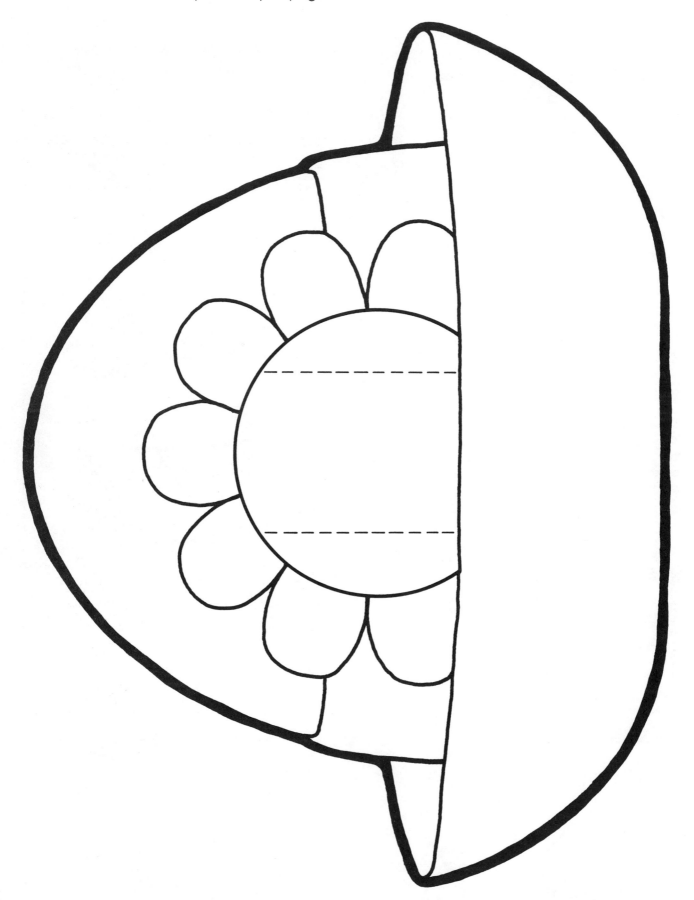

H Pattern
Use with the "Create A Hat" activity on page 53.

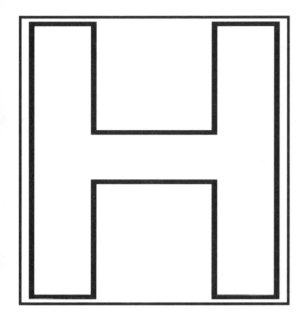

Hat Word Card
Use with the "Hat Tachistoscope" activity on page 54.

H Picture Strips
Use with the "Hat Tachistoscope" activity on page 54.

Glue to the other strip.

heart

hanger

house

horse

Pull here.

helicopter

hammer

hippo

hand

Pull here.

I is for insects

Incredible insects abound in this interesting unit.

Who's Who Insect Poem

Prepare all of the insect pictures, except the ladybug, on page 65 for flannelboard use to accompany the poem.

1. Insect in the grass,
   Insect in the hay,
   Insect in the weeds
   Hops around all day.
   (a grasshopper)

2. Insect in the dirt,
   Insect in the sand,
   Insect in the rocks
   Crawls upon my hand.
   (an ant)

3. Insect in the sky,
   Insect in my hair,
   Insect in the clouds
   Flies up in the air.
   (a butterfly)

4. Insect in a hive,
   Insect with some fuzz,
   Insect on a flower
   Zooms by with a buzz.
   (a bee)

Butterfly Insect Snack

Help your youngsters metamorphose some simple ingredients into interesting insect snacks. Cut a slice of bread twice diagonally into four triangles; use two of the triangles for butterfly wings. Spread the bread with softened cream cheese. Arrange the triangle wings on a plate with a small carrot or celery stick body and a mini-marshmallow head. Let your youngsters decorate the wings with raisins and sunflower seeds or with any kind of colorful dry cereal.

"Insects"

Sing this to the tune of "A Bicycle Built for Two."

Insects, insects,
You are so very small.
Insects, insects,
Sometimes I see you crawl.

You fly and you buzz right by.
You jump up in the sky.
You are so small, the smallest of all,
Little insect friends of mine.

Insect Booklet Page

Use the *I* booklet page on page 62 as directed for previous letters. Have your youngsters draw and color one or more insects within the jar illustration. Write each child's dictation within the space provided above the jar.

Brilliant Butterflies

Reproduce the pattern on page 63 to make a butterfly-shaped tagboard tracer. Trace a full butterfly shape on white construction paper for each child. Have your youngsters design their butterfly wings by coloring circles, ovals, and other shapes within the outline. Have them color these shapes with very heavy crayon. Brush over the colored butterflies with water-thinned tempera paint to create a crayon resist design. Cut out the dry butterflies and glue thin paper antennae to the heads.

Interesting Insect Cage

Constructing this little insect cage is easy enough for even your youngest students. Reproduce the insect cage pattern on page 64 on light brown construction paper. Reproduce the patterns on page 65 on white construction paper, color, and cut out.

Carefully cut out the triangle piece on the cage. Attach the picture wheel to the cage at the ○ using a brad. Glue the block letter *I* to the cage above the words "is for insect." Let each student glue her choice of insect pictures to the cage, leaving the picture wheel opening uncovered.

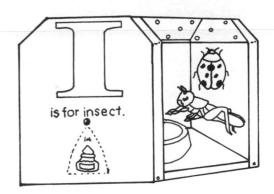

is for insect.

Backyard Insects
by Millicent E. Selsam and Ronald Goor

- Have your youngsters list the names of insects they have seen, using the book as a guide. Let your students take turns circling all of the *I*s in the insect names.

- Choose some well-known insects from the story such as caterpillars, butterflies, and bees. Let small groups of students imitate these insects, demonstrating how they move.

- Ask each youngster to choose an insect from the book to use as the subject for a story titled "My Favorite Insect." Use the insect cage pattern on page 64, masking the words and the cut-out space on the left side. Reproduce the cage on white construction paper. Write each child's dictated story in the open space on the left side of the page. Have each youngster draw and color her insect, cut it out, and glue it to the screen area of the cage.

Interesting Insect Books

Bugs by Nancy Winslow Parker and Joan Richards Wright
Insect World by Time-Life Books

More Insect and *I* Activities

- Have the students complete the "Insects Are In" activity sheet on page 66.

- Make insect finger-puppets using the insect patterns on page 65.

- Explain to the children that they have a finger-print pattern on each finger that is unique. Have the children use the flat side of their pencil lead to color a thick, black area. Press their finger on this penciled area and cover the finger with clear tape. Pull off the tape and stick it on paper. Allow the children to add a head, antennae, and six legs with a permanent marker to make finger-print insects.

- Make a display of plastic insects available at toy stores or specialty shops. Arrange the insects in natural settings around the classroom such as on a plant, a window, or your shoulder.

- Bring in squeeze-tube icing and have each child print his name on paper. Allow them to dry and hang these masterpieces on a bulletin board titled "Sweet Kids."

- Serve your students ice cream in a paper cup as a sweet *I* snack.

Insects

Insects are in a jar. There is a

Pattern
Use with the "Brilliant Butterflies"
activity on page 60.

Place on fold.

Pattern
Insect Cage

Use with the "Interesting Insect Cage" activity and the third *Backyard Insects* activity on page 61.

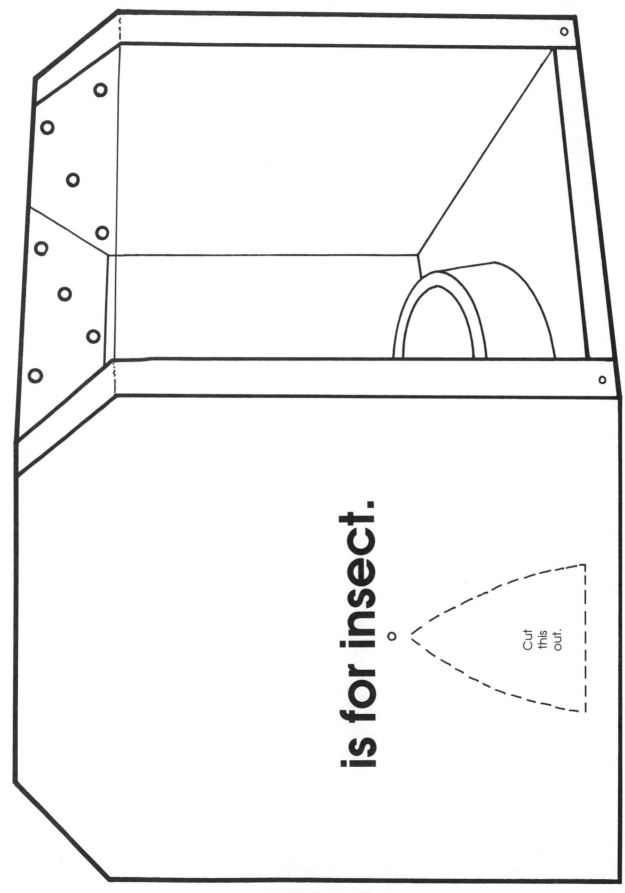

is for insect.

Cut
this
out.

Use with the "Interesting Insect Cage" activity on page 61.

Use the insects (except the ladybug) with the "Who's Who Insect Poem" activity on page 60. Use all the insects with the second "More *I* Activities" activity on page 61.

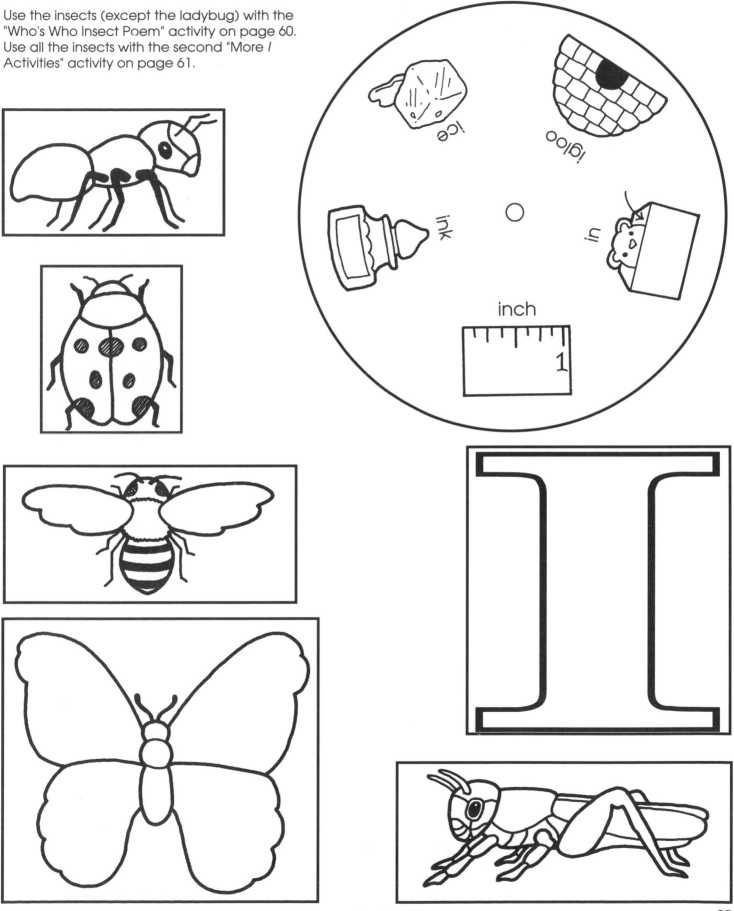

inch

igloo

ice

ink

in

1

Name _____

Insects Are In!

Color.
Cut and paste.
Put each insect **in** a container.

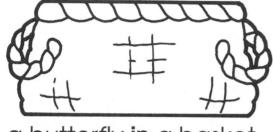

a butterfly **in** a basket

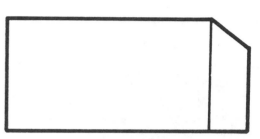

a ladybug **in** a box

a caterpillar **in** a cup

a bee **in** a bag

J is for jacket

Try these jacket activities on for size.

A Jacket For Me

Use the jacket illustration on the jacket booklet page (page 69) to make a jacket flash card for each color you use in the poem.

J-a-c, k-e-t!
Here's a [red] jacket
Just for me.

J-a-c, k-e-t!
Here's a [blue] jacket
Just for me.

As you repeat the three basic lines in the poem, replace the color word in line two with a different color.

Jam Jackets

Construct yummy jackets from bread and jam! Cut a one-inch-wide piece off the bottom of a slice of bread. Cut this piece in half to form two sleeve pieces. Use the remaining large piece of bread for the jacket body. Position the jacket body piece on a paper plate or napkin. Position the two sleeve pieces extending out from the sides of the jacket body. Spread the bread jacket with jam and top it with diced fruit buttons.

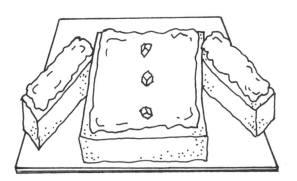

"Jacket Pockets"

Bring "Twinkle, Twinkle, Little Star" down to earth with this hidden surprise song.

Jacket pockets are so neat; they can hold a special treat.
In a pocket, things can hide.
Hide [a cupcake] way inside.
Jacket pockets are so neat; they can hold a special treat.

Repeat the song and replace the object each time with another item such as *an apple, a cookie,* and *some raisins.* Pull each item (or a picture of the item) out of your jacket pocket as you name it.

Jacket Booklet Page

Use the *J* booklet page on page 69 as directed for previous letters. Have your youngsters color their jacket illustrations as desired. Write each child's dictation within the space provided to describe the times she may wear it.

Jazzy Jackets

This jacket portrait project will jazz up any bulletin board. Begin by reproducing the jacket portrait pattern on page 70 on white construction paper. Have each youngster color a jacket and add details with glitter, dimensional paint, or sequins. Give each youngster a thin paper plate to decorate with crayon facial features and construction-paper or yarn hair. Cut out the jacket around the bold outline. Glue or staple the paper plate portrait to the jacket neckline where indicated. Display your students' work on a bulletin board titled "Our Jazzy Jackets."

67

Fold-Open Jacket

This little jacket project should fit your youngsters' learning needs. Reproduce the jacket patterns on pages 71 and 72 on colored construction paper. Have your youngsters cut out the two jacket front pieces and the jacket backing piece. Staple the two front pieces to the backing at the sides where indicated. Reproduce the patterns on page 73 on white construction paper. Color, cut out, and glue the pockets to the jacket fronts where indicated. Color, cut out, and glue the letter *J* to the jacket front. Cut out the picture cards and store them in the jacket pockets.

Have youngsters select a picture card, say its name, and place it in one of the spaces on the jacket backing. Add extra distractor cards programmed with pictures that begin with other letters, if desired.

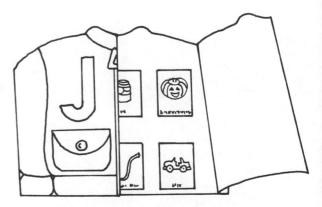

The Jacket I Wear In The Snow
by Shirley Neitzel

- Carefully study the jacket illustration on the first page. Have your youngsters list the features of this cozy jacket (zipper, snaps at the neck, quilting, etc.). After making the list, have them tell you why these features make this an appropriate jacket for snowy weather.

- Have your youngsters describe, in their own words, the sequence of preparation for the child's time in the snow. Ask them to decide why the child was so unhappy with her clothes. Have them decide on just a *few* garments, along with the jacket, that the child could wear for a shorter but perhaps happier and more comfortable playtime in the snow.

- The jacket in the story was perfect for a snowy winter day. Have your youngsters describe different jackets that would be suitable for a windy autumn day, a rainy spring day, or a foggy summer morning at the beach. Have each student draw his idea of one of these jackets, then title his work "The Jacket I Wear In The [Snow, Wind, Rain, Fog]."

More Jacket Books

Drip Drop by Sharon Gordon
My First Look At Clothes from Random House Publishers
Peter Rabbit by Beatrix Potter
The Snowy Day by Ezra Jack Keats

More Jacket and *J* Activities

- Make a human bar graph with your students. Have each child wear his jacket and work as a class to line up according to color in graph form. Transfer human-graph numbers to large square graph paper. Try other categories such as jackets with hoods, jackets without hoods, jackets with pockets and jackets without pockets.

- Cut out a large jacket shape from bulletin board paper. Cut *J*-shaped sponges and have the students print *J*s on the jacket with tempera paint.

- Make a list of boys' and girls' names that begin with the letter *J*. Have each student with a name on the list come up and circle his name.

- Have a jumping contest. Mark a starting line on the floor. Have each child toe the line and then jump forward as far as he can. Explain to the children that you are going to measure the length of each student's jump with a yardstick. Involve the students in measuring their own length and record the lengths on a chart.

- Recite the jacket poem on page 67 as you and your youngsters jump rope.

- Serve a yummy *J* snack of assorted jams and jellies on graham crackers.

Jacket

This is my jacket. I wear it when

Pattern
Jacket Portrait
Use with the "Jazzy Jackets" activity on page 67.

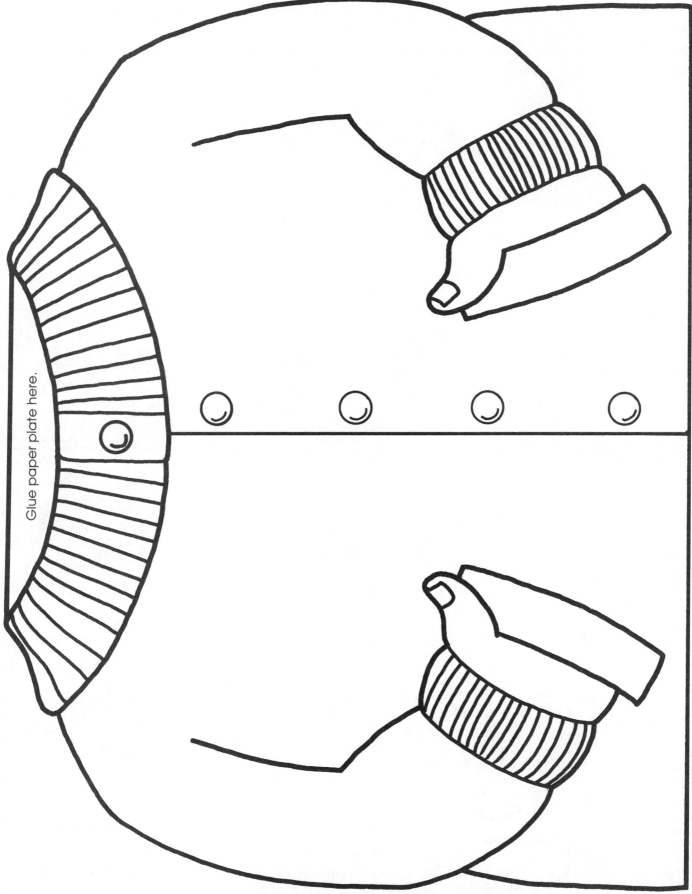

Glue paper plate here.

right
jacket
front

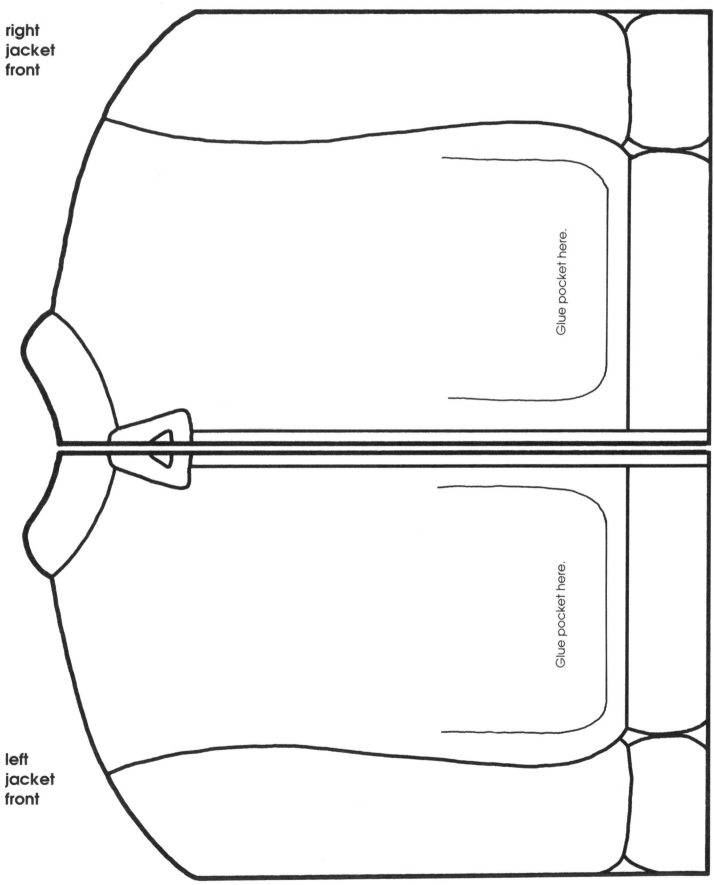

Glue pocket here.

Glue pocket here.

left
jacket
front

Pattern
Jacket Backing
Use with the "Fold-Open Jacket" activity on page 68.

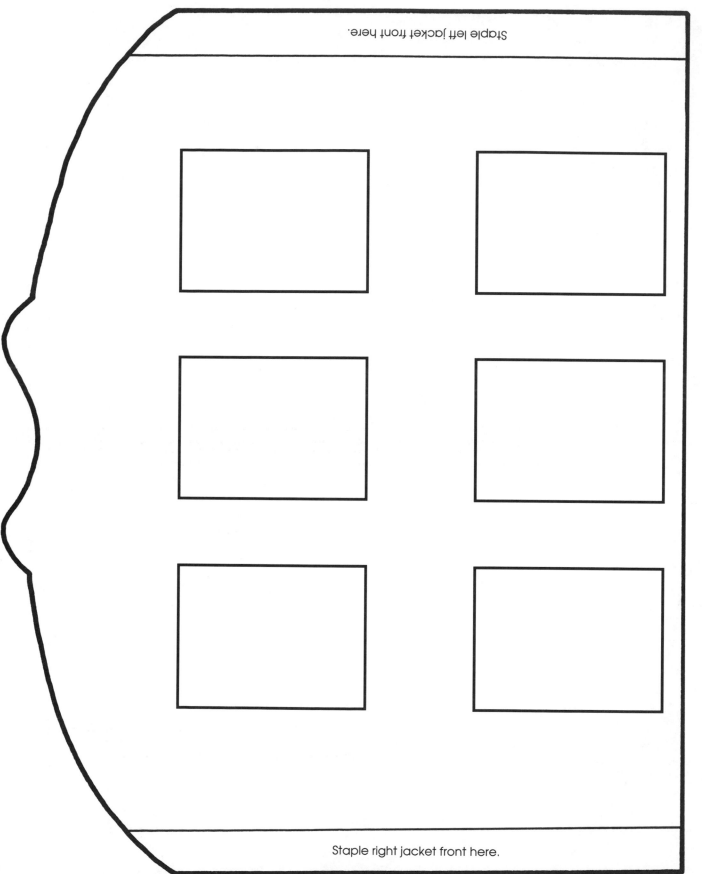

Staple left jacket front here.

Staple right jacket front here.

pockets

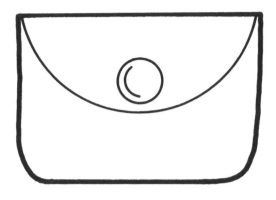

J **for jacket**

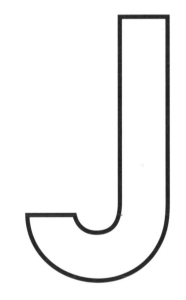

picture cards

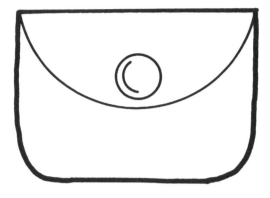

jar

jack-o'-lantern

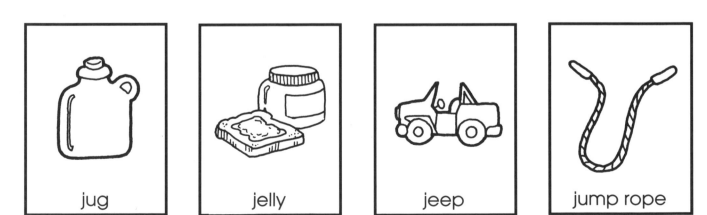

jug

jelly

jeep

jump rope

K is for kangaroo

Teaching these *K* activities will have your class hopping!

The Kangaroo Hop

Your youngsters will jump at the chance to learn this bouncy poem.

Verse 1   Hop, hop, hop on two big feet.
                  Baby in her pocket so tidy and neat.

Chorus   Hop, hop, hop in the sun and rain.
                  Kan-ga, Kan-ga-roo is her name.

Verse 2   Hop, hop, hop on two big feet.
                  Green, green grass she likes to eat.

Repeat chorus.

Verse 3   Hop, hop, hop on two big feet.
                  She can hop right over the street.

Repeat chorus.

Kangaroo Pockets

Cut round pocket bread in half to make two half pockets. Provide one half pocket for each child to stuff with his favorite fillings such as peanut butter, cheese, egg salad, tuna salad, or cream cheese.

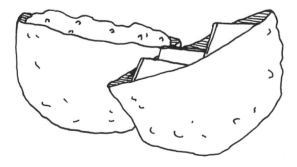

"K-A-N-G-A!"

Sing this song to the tune of "B-I-N-G-O."

Verse   There is a kangaroo I know and Kanga is her name-O.
Chorus   K-A-N-G-A, K-A-N-G-A,
           K-A-N-G-A, and Kangaroo's her name-O.

Repeat the verse, changing it to:
        There is a kangaroo that [hops] and Kanga is her name-O.

Replace the verb in the verse with a new verb such as *jumps, skips,* or *leaps* each time you repeat the verse.

Kangaroo Booklet Page

Use the kangaroo booklet page on page 76 as directed for previous letters. Have your youngsters draw something sticking out of the kangaroo's pocket. Write each child's dictation within the space provided in the lower right corner of the page.

Kangaroo's Kites

Use the kangaroo patterns on pages 78, 79, and 80 to make a large bulletin-board kangaroo character. Reproduce the pieces on tan construction paper, cut them out, and glue them together. Add a black felt-pen nose. Display it on a bulletin board titled "Kangaroo's Kites." Provide each of your youngsters with the kite and kite tail patterns on page 77, reproduced on white construction paper. Have each student draw an object that begins with *K* within each of the three empty triangle spaces on the kite. Cut out the kites and pin them to the bulletin board. Connect each kite to the kangaroo's paw with a length of string. Pin each child's three kite tail pieces to the string of the kite.

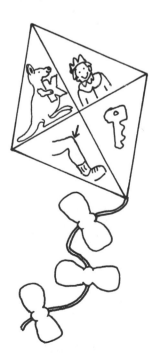

Kanga's *K* Pocket

Reproduce the patterns on pages 78, 79, and 80 on white construction paper. Have your youngsters color each piece and cut it out. Glue the top and bottom halves of the kangaroo together. Attach the arm and the tail to the kangaroo with brads. Glue the pocket on the kangaroo where shown. Cut out the *K* picture cards and store them in the kangaroo's pocket. To use, have students take the cards out of the kangaroo's pocket and say the name of the picture on each card.

Katy No-Pocket
by Emmy Payne

• Poor mother Katy Kangaroo had no pocket to carry her baby! Ask your youngsters to consider why Katy has no pocket, while all the other mothers do! Discuss the features that she does have in common with the other kangaroos.

• Katy found a man with lots of pockets who could help her. Have your youngsters decide what his job was and discuss what *he* kept in the pockets. Have them speculate what the man did with his tools after he gave his pocket apron to Katy. Let your youngsters tell you what they would keep in an apron with so many pockets.

• Thankfully Katy did finally get all the pockets she could use! Have students list other items that a mother kangaroo could keep in a pocket in a fantasy story. Circle all of the letter *K*s that appear in your youngsters' list of items.

Kangaroo Tales

Big Talk by Miriam Schlein
It's Not Fair! by Anita Harper
Joey Runs Away by Jack Kent
Norma Jean, Jumping Bean by Joanna Cole
Play Ball, Joey Kangaroo! by Donna Lugg Pape

More Kangaroo And *K* Activities

• Explain to the children that kangaroos are not the only animals that have a pouch. Show students pictures of an opossum and a koala. These two animals also have pouches but use them only a short time to carry their young. Tell the children that baby kangaroos are called joeys and stay in their mother's pouch for up to a year. Have the students name other animals and the names of their babies.

• Wear a carpenter's apron with many pockets and fill them with objects that begin with *K*. Allow children to come up one at a time, choose an item from a pocket, and say the name of the item. Reinforce the *K* sound of each word. Encourage children to bring items that start with *K* and would fit into a pocket.

• Set out keys of many shapes and sizes. Have your students trace around the keys or place them under paper to make a crayon rubbing.

• Hang a real kite from your wall or ceiling. Have children cut out the letter *K* or pictures from magazines that begin with the letter *K* and glue them on the kite.

• Form a circle with your students and play kangaroo kick. Have students kick the ball from person to person, keeping the ball inside the circle.

• Kiss your students with a Hersheys™ Kiss glued to good work.

• Serve Kix™ cereal for a kicky snack.

Kangaroo

Kanga has a
big pocket!

Inside
her pocket
is a

Patterns

Use with the "Kangaroo's Kites" activity on page 74 and the "Kanga's *K* Pocket" activity on page 75.

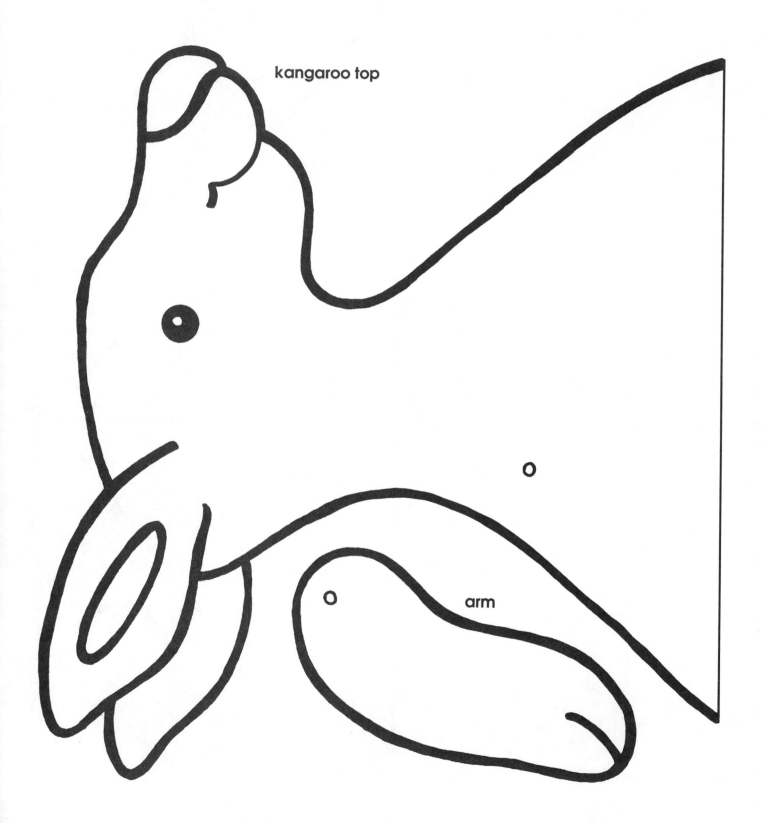

kangaroo top

arm

Patterns

Use with the "Kangaroo's Kites" activity on page 74 and the "Kanga's *K* Pocket" activity on page 75.

kangaroo bottom

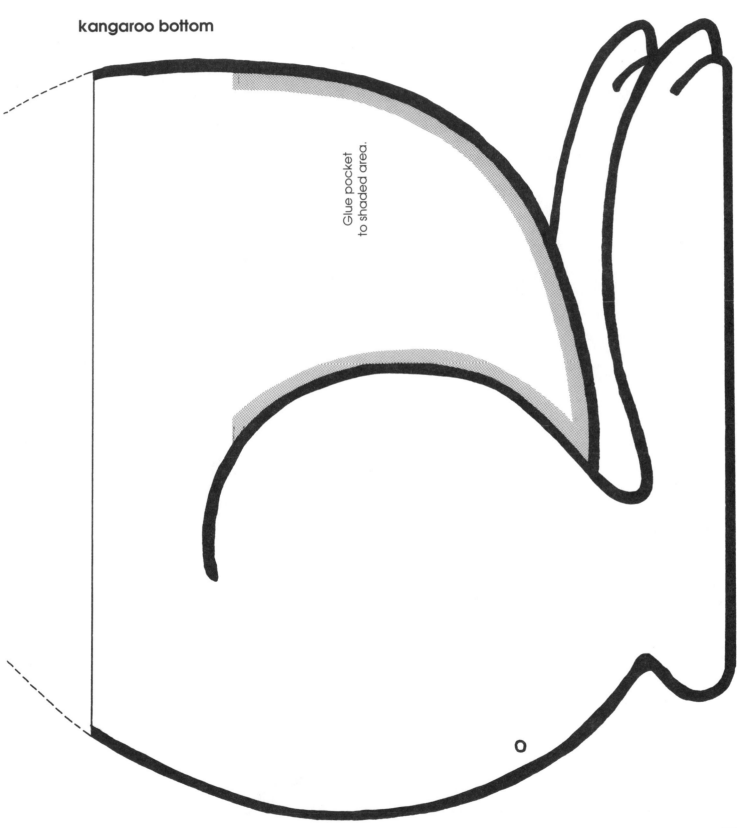

Glue pocket to shaded area.

o

Patterns

Use with the "Kangaroo's Kites" activity on page 74 and the "Kanga's *K* Pocket" activity on page 75.

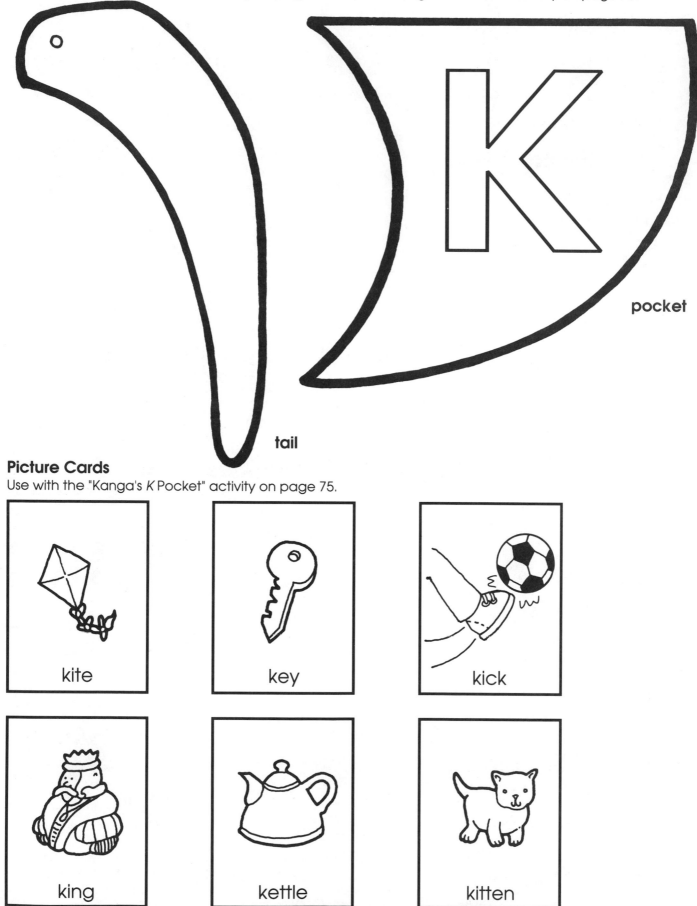

pocket

tail

Picture Cards

Use with the "Kanga's *K* Pocket" activity on page 75.

| kite | key | kick |
| king | kettle | kitten |

L is for lion

Learning is easy when smilin' lions teach the letter *L*.

"One Little Lion"

Have your youngsters perform the action for each line.

> One little lion went out to play.
> *(Show one with pointer finger.)*
> He said, "I will [run] today."
> *(Point to self.)*
> So he [ran] and [ran] and [ran] around.
> *(Run in place.)*
> Now he's the sleepiest lion in town!
> *(Pretend to sleep.)*

Replace the action words *ran/run* with new action words each time such as *swim/swam, jump/jumped, walk/walked,* and *dance/danced.*

A Lion Lunch

Make a luscious lion with a few simple ingredients. Spread a mini rice cake with peanut butter. Have each youngster press grated cheddar cheese into the peanut butter around the circumference of the rice cake to make the lion's mane. Cut lunch meat into small triangles, and use one triangle for the nose and two triangles for the ears. Finish the lion's face with toasted ◯-shaped cereal eyes.

"I'm A Little Lion"

Sing this song to the tune of "I'm A Little Teapot." Let your youngsters *roar* at the end.

> I'm a little lion
> On the plain.
> Here is my tail and
> Here is my mane.
> When I get excited
> You will see
> Just how loud
> My roar can be!

Lion Booklet Page

Use the lion booklet page on page 83 as directed for previous letters. Have your youngsters draw something under the lion to show what he is lying on. Write each child's dictation within the space provided to describe the lion's sleeping spot.

Lion Disguises

Little ones like to pretend, and your youngsters will enjoy being disguised as lions. Reproduce the lion mask pattern on page 84 on tagboard. Have your students sponge-print the masks with light brown or yellow tempera paint and let them dry. Cut along all of the dotted lines with an X-acto knife. Let your youngsters glue yellow and brown tissue- or crepe-paper strips along the top edge and sides of the masks to form manes. Reproduce the ear patterns on page 85 on white construction paper. Color, cut out, and snip along the slash marks. Fold each ear on the line and glue the slashed section to the mask where indicated. Cut an inch-wide tagboard strip for each child for a headband. Staple the band to the mask where indicated, fitting the headband to the child.

Lion Foldout Book

Make a lengthy lion book that's long on *L* words. Reproduce the lion pattern on page 86 on yellow construction paper. Reproduce the foldout page patterns on page 87 on white construction paper. Have each child complete each page with a phrase and an illustration in the spaces provided. Cut out the lion pieces and the letter *L* on page 86 and the foldout pages on page 87. Glue the pages to the lion front and back where indicated. Glue the *L* to the back end of the lion. Fold the book up accordion style.

A Lion For Lewis
by Rosemary Wells

- Sophie and George were very bossy to Lewis. Have your youngsters discuss why they were so bossy to him. Ask three volunteers to act out the parts of the children in the story. Help the child playing the part of Lewis say things to convince the others to let him have a turn being boss. Be sure that each child gets a turn to pretend.

- The attic in the story contained lots of fun items for playing pretend. Have your youngsters decide where the lion came from and what it was originally used for.

- Have your students brainstorm a list of words to describe how Lewis felt before he found the lion suit. Then have them generate a contrasting list of words describing how Lewis felt after he put the lion suit on.

Lion Literature

Clemens' Kingdom by Chris L. Demarest
Eli by Bill Peet
Lazy Lion by Mwenye Hadithi
The Loudest Little Lion by Joy Elizabeth Hancock
So Hungry! by Harriet Ziefert

More Lion And *L* Activities

- Introduce the children to the lion family by naming each member. The father is called a *lion*. The mother is called a *lioness*. The babies are called *cubs* and a group of lions is called a *pride*. Children are always amazed at the fact that it is the mother lion who hunts food for the family.

- Fill a large jar with lollipops. Have your students estimate how many lollipops are in the jar. Count them together as a class. Give a lollipop to the student with the closest estimate.

- Write *My name is Lollipop Lion and I like_____* on a chart. Explain to the students that you need to fill in the missing word but it can only start with the letter *L*. Have each student come up and repeat the sentence, adding his own *L* word in the blank. Allow him to choose a lollipop from the estimation jar as he sits down. Write each student's *L* word on the bottom of the chart paper.

- Have students bring in leaves. Glue them to a large tagboard cutout tree and title it "Lots of Lovely Leaves."

- Show the children how the index finger and thumb of the left hand makes the *L* shape. This will help them remember which hand is their left hand.

- Give each student several animal crackers and have him sort the crackers into separate animal piles. Count the total number of lion crackers found in the class. Serve the youngsters a cup of "lion-ade" (lemonade) to drink while munching on the crackers.

Lion

The lion is lying on a

Pattern
Lion Mask

Use with the "Lion Disguises" activity on page 81.

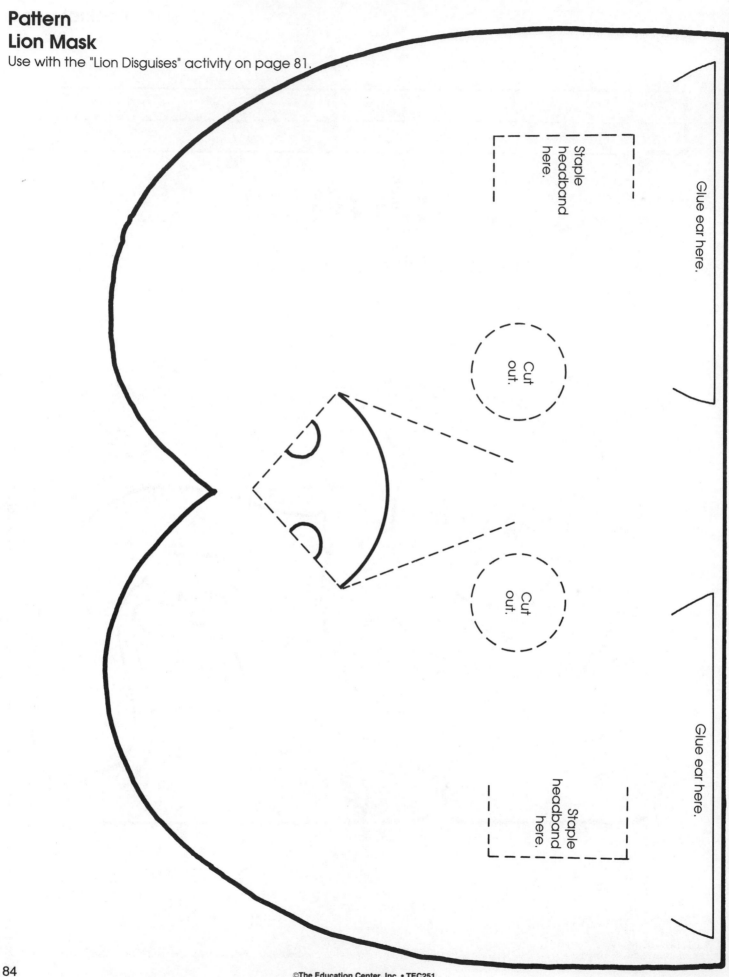

Glue ear here.

Staple headband here.

Cut out.

Cut out.

Staple headband here.

Glue ear here.

ears

Fold here.

Fold here.

Parent Note
Use upon completion of letter *L* activities.

There's no denyin'; I'm not lyin'!

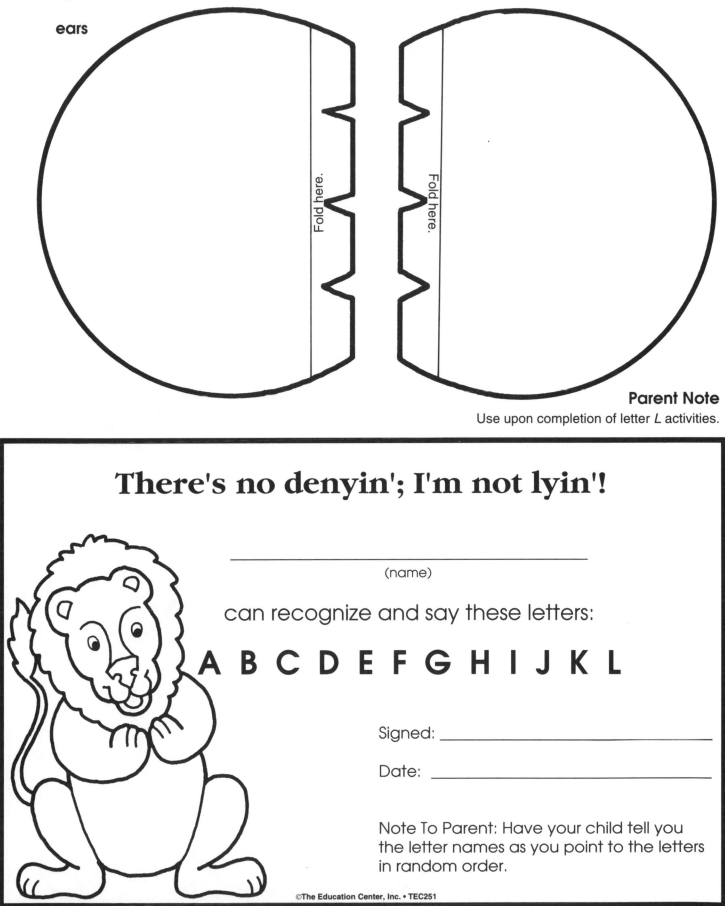

_____
(name)

can recognize and say these letters:

A B C D E F G H I J K L

Signed: _____

Date: _____

Note To Parent: Have your child tell you the letter names as you point to the letters in random order.

Pattern
Foldout Book Covers

Use with the "Lion Foldout Book" activity on page 82.

L lion

back

Glue
L here.

front

Glue to the back of the lion.

Lion laughs at

Lion learns about

Lion leaps over

Lion lies on

Glue to the other strip.

Glue to the front of the lion.

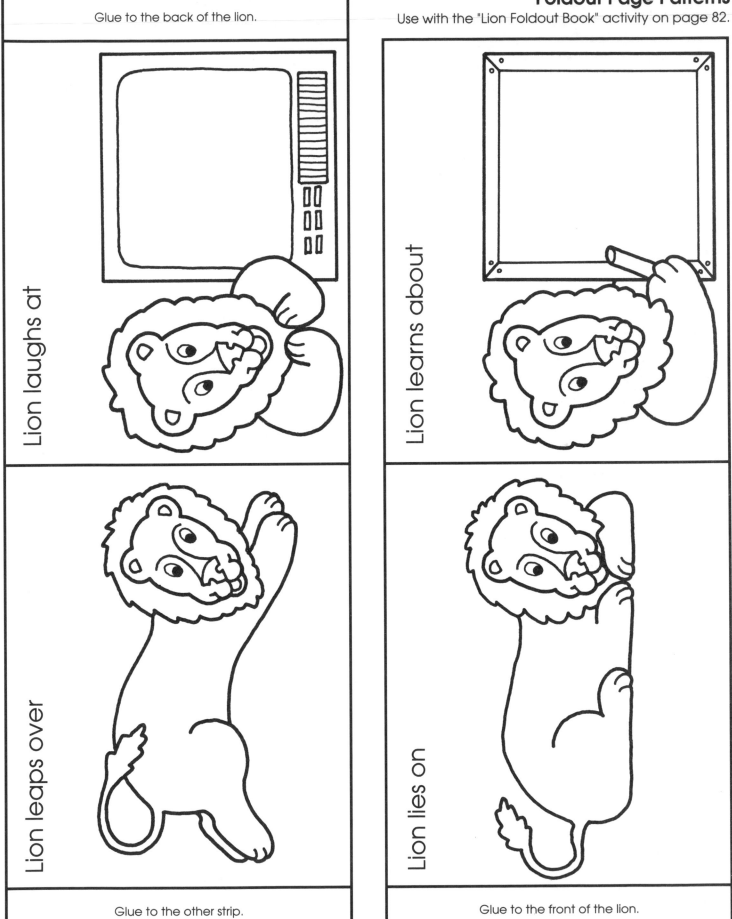

M is for mouse

With mice every day, learning *M* is play!

"Once There Was A Little Mouse"

Encourage youngsters to have fun with the movements that accompany this poem.

Once there was a little mouse,
   (Show little *with thumb and pointer finger.)*
Who lived inside a little house.
   (Join fingertips to form a slanted roof.)
He had a twitchy little nose. *(Twitch nose.)*
He had some furry little toes. *(Wiggle toes.)*
He had some whiskers, long and thin.
   (Pretend to stroke whiskers.)
He had a funny little grin. *(Smile.)*
He had a great big appetite. *(Rub tummy.)*
He ate up all the cheese in sight!
   (Pretend to gobble food.)

A Cheesy Mouse Treat

Sculpt your favorite cheese ball recipe into a mouse shape and create a yummy snack. Prepare the cheese ball ingredients as your recipe directs. Sculpt these ingredients into a rounded, wedge-shaped mouse and carefully roll it in finely chopped nuts. Cut two ears from cheese and press them into the sides of the mouse's head area. Slice a pimento-filled green olive to make two eyes. Press a small black olive into the front of the mouse for a nose. Add a strand of cooked spaghetti to the opposite end for a tail. Serve this cheesy mouse with an assortment of your favorite crackers.

"Where Is Mousekin?"

Sing this song to the tune of "Frère Jacqué."

   Where is Mousekin? Where is Mousekin?
   Here I am! Here I am!
   Can you [twirl your tail], Sir?
   Very well, I thank you!
   Run away; run away.

Repeat the song. Replace the action in line three with a new action each time you sing the verse. Use "twitch your nose," "show your teeth," "wave your ears," or "eat some cheese."

Mouse Booklet Page

Use the *M* booklet page on page 90 as directed for previous letters. Have each of your youngsters think of something for the mouse to munch; then have him draw a picture of it atop the mouse's extended paw. Write each child's dictation in the space provided to describe the mouse's munchie!

Mouse Bag Puppet

Reproduce the mouse face and paw patterns on page 91 on white construction paper. Let each child color her pattern pieces, adding eyes and whiskers to the upper portion of the mouse's head. Provide each child with a small, folded paper lunch bag. Cut out the upper portion of the head and glue it to the bag flap, aligning the straight edges. Cut out the lower portion of the head and glue it beneath the flap of the bag. Cut out the paws and glue them to the bag.

Mouse's Belongings Book

A child who makes this little book may just be inspired to learn to read! Each child will need a copy of the backing piece on page 92 reproduced on tagboard and a copy of pages 93 and 94 reproduced on white construction paper. Have each child color his backing piece and cut it out on the bold outline. Have him color the objects on each half page and then dictate a few words to complete the sentence starter below each object. Repeat the process for the mask illustration on the lower half of the backing piece. Cut the half pages out and stack them together, placing them on the bottom half of the backing piece. Staple the pages to the backing piece along the left side.

If You Give A Mouse A Cookie
by Laura Joffe Numeroff

- Have your youngsters speculate what the mouse was doing and where he was going when he met the boy. Have them list things that might have been in the mouse's backpack.

- The mouse was delighted to get a cookie from the boy. Have your youngsters make a list of foods that begin with *M* that the mouse might enjoy. Let each student take a turn at completing the following sentence with a word from the *M* list and her own creative ending: "If you give a mouse a _____, he'll _____."

- Bring in objects from the story that were paired together such as a straw and a glass, a sponge and a pail, a puff and a powder box, crayons and paper, and a cookie and a small plate. Store all of the objects in a box and have pairs of students take turns sorting through and pairing up the objects.

Marvelous Mouse Books

Mouse Count and *Mouse Paint* by Ellen Stoll Walsh
Four Brave Sailors by Mirra Ginsburg
Frederick by Leo Lionni
The Little Mouse, The Red Ripe Strawberry, And The Big Hungry Bear by Don and Audrey Wood
Norman The Doorman by Don Freeman

More Mouse And *M* Activities

- Collect pictures of animals whose names begin with *M* such as moose, muskrat, manatee, marmot, mink, mongoose, and man. Help the children become familiar with and recognize some of these unusual animals.

- Explain to the children there are many types of music and one type of music is called a march. Play a march selection and ask the students how the music makes them feel. Show the children how to march and march together around the room while the music plays.

- Fill two identical jars with marshmallows; one with large and one with small. Ask the children which jar has more marshmallows. Open the jars and count the marshmallows in each jar. Have the youngsters hypothesize why there are more in one jar than in the other.

- Use the marshmallows in the previous activity to make marshmallow men. Give the students an assortment of marshmallows to glue onto construction paper in the shape of a man. Use crayons to color in the background.

- Introduce the children to different denominations of money.

- Use a mixer to make muffins and eat them as a snack.

M   m

Mouse

The mouse wanted to munch! He munched on

Finished
Bag
Puppet

Pattern
Backing Piece
Use with the "Mouse's Belongings Book" activity on page 89.

If You Give A Mouse

Staple pages here.

a mask, he will

Use with the "Mouse's Belongings Book" activity on page 89.

some mittens, he will

a muffin, he will

hole

cat

cheese

boot

a map, he will

IN MICE   WE TRUST

1   1

some money, he will

N is for nest

This nest egg of *N* activities is full of fun.

Nice Nest Poem

Let your youngsters work as a group to make up movements for each line of the poem.

1. Here is the nest
   All safe and warm.
   Here's where the chicks
   Are safe from harm.

2. Here is the nest
   All hidden away.
   Here's where the chicks
   Can safely play.

3. Here is the nest
   All cozy and deep.
   Here's where the chicks
   Are fast asleep.

Bird Nest Cookies

These old-time favorites are also known as Thumbprint Cookies.

Mix thoroughly:
    1/2 cup soft shortening (half butter)
    1/4 cup packed brown sugar
    1 egg yolk (Reserve the white.)
    1/2 teaspoon vanilla

Sift together and stir in:
    1 cup sifted flour
    1/4 teaspoon salt

Mix the dough well. Roll the dough into one-inch balls. Dip each ball into slightly beaten egg white and then roll in shredded coconut. Place each ball on a cookie sheet; then push down the center with your thumb to make a nest shape with a depression in the center. Bake the cookies at 375 degrees for 10 to 12 minutes and let them cool. Let each child choose a jelly bean "egg" to place inside his cookie nest.

"I Spy A Nest"

This nifty song takes its tune from "Old MacDonald Had A Farm."

I spy a nest up in a tree. Way up, way up high.
And in that nest what can there be? Way up, way up high.
There's a [robin] there, way up in the air.
Way up high, in the sky.
In the nest that I spy.
I spy a nest up in a tree. Way up, way up high!

Each time that you sing line three, replace the bird name with a new one. Use two-syllable names such as *blue jay, sparrow,* and *blue-bird.*

Nest Booklet Page

Use the *N* booklet page on page 97 as directed for previous letters. Have each child glue on construction-paper scraps cut in thin strips to create a nest under the hen. Write each child's dictation in the space provided to complete the sentence starter.

Nest Catchall Project

Reproduce the two nest patterns on page 98 on white construction paper. Have your youngsters color the nests and cut them out. Provide each child with a brown paper lunch bag. Roll down the top of the bag to create a rolled rim and a sack height of about five inches. Glue one nest shape to each side of the bag. Write each child's name on her nest shapes. Let your students use their nest catchalls to store school supplies.

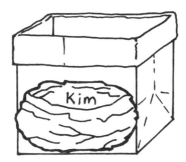

Nifty Nest Tachistoscope

Building a nifty nest will be child's play when you provide your students with the patterns on pages 99, 100, and 101. Reproduce all three pattern pages on white construction paper. Have your youngsters color the two nest pages and the chicks, then cut them out along the bold lines. Carefully slit the dotted lines on the nest tachistoscope page and glue the chicks inside the nest. Stack the *N* page on top of the tachistoscope page and staple them together at the top. Cut out the two picture strips and help your students glue them together where indicated. Thread the strip through the slits. To use, pull the strip to reveal each picture.

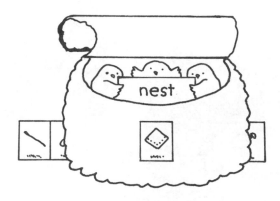

Have You Seen My Duckling?
by Nancy Tafuri

- Ask your students to carefully study the nest illustration on the title page. Have them brainstorm a list of materials that the nest might be made of. Have them discuss how the ducklings feel when they are inside the nest.

- Look at the two pages showing the mother duck approaching the nest. Have your students describe the environment where the duck has built the nest. Have them decide why she has hidden the nest away in the plants.

- Have your youngsters name each animal that the duck family encounters in their search. Write down their names on the blackboard or on chart paper (heron, beaver, fish, turtle, frog, crayfish, water bug, salamander, and merganser). Discuss which animals do build nests or nestlike structures.

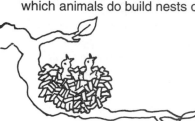

Nifty Nest Books

A First Look At Bird Nests by Millicent Ellis Selsam and Joyce Hunt
Are You My Mother? by P. D. Eastman
Birds And Their Nests by Gwynne Vevers Burks
Window Into A Nest by Geraldine Lux Flanagan

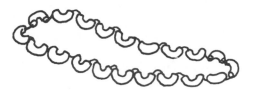

More Nest and *N* Activities

- Make a list of all boys' and girls' names that begin with or contain the letter *N*. Have each named student circle the *N* found in his name with a marker.

- Have your students string a necklace of noodles by using yarn and uncooked macaroni noodles. These necklaces can be painted with watercolors or glitter can be glued onto the noodles.

- Make newspaper nests by cutting thin strips of newspaper and helping children glue them into coffee filters.

- Introduce the children to the nickel coin. Allow children to look at a nickel while discussing the pictures on each side and the amount of money it is worth. Have each child glue the nickel to a sheet of unlined paper and draw what he might buy with that nickel.

- Have the children form numerals out of cooked spagetti noodles.

- Serve a delicious nest snack of Chinese noodles. Allow the children to arrange the noodles in a nest shape and drop in a candy egg.

Nest

Nellie needs a nest! I'll make a nest out of

Patterns

Use with the "Nest Catchall Project" activity on page 95.

Pattern
***Nn* Nest**

Use with the "Nifty Nest Tachistoscope" activity on page 96.

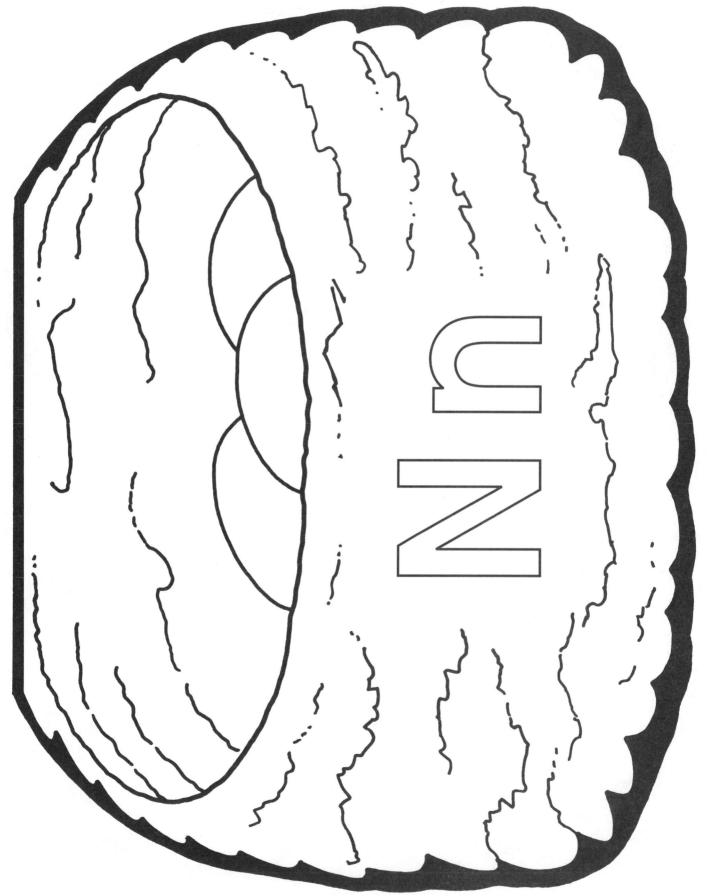

Pattern
Nest Tachistoscope

Use with the "Nifty Nest Tachistoscope" activity on page 96.

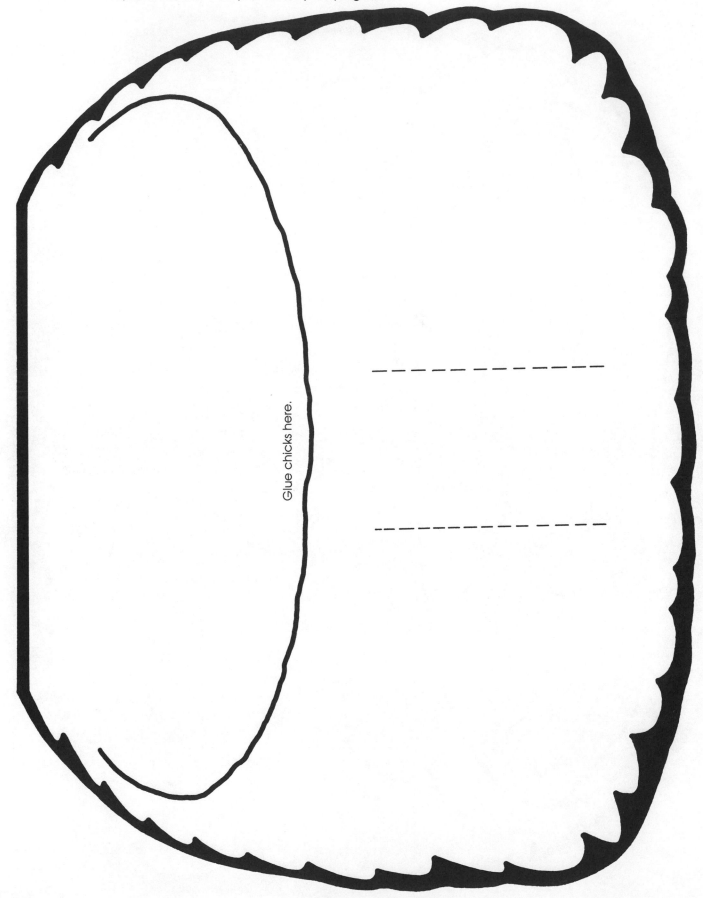

Glue chicks here.

Use with the "Nifty Nest Tachistoscope" activity on page 96.

picture strips

chicks

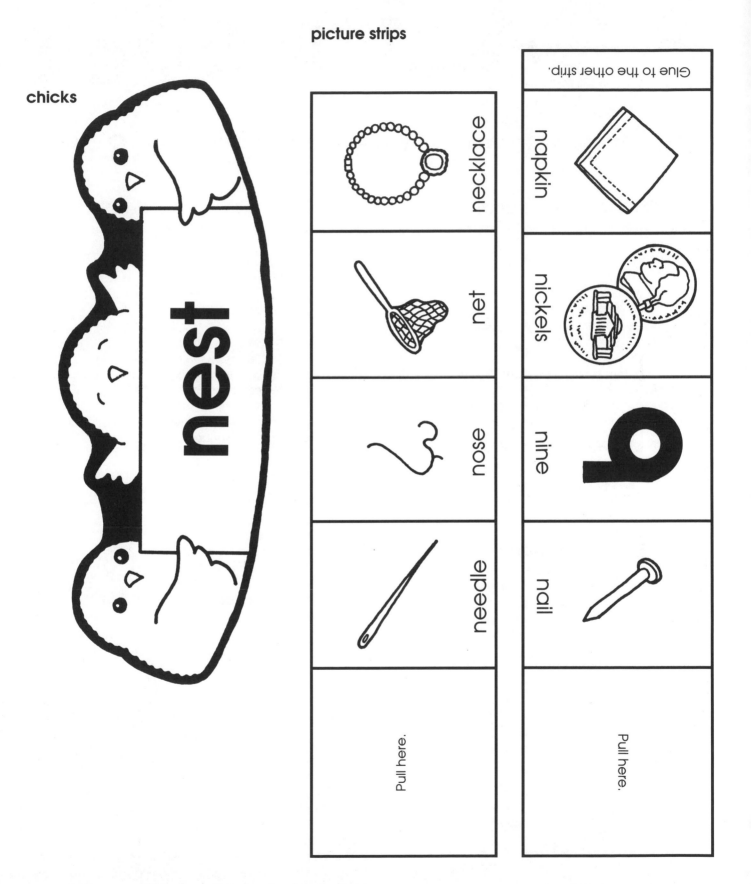

nest

necklace

net

nose

needle

Pull here.

Glue to the other strip.

napkin

nickels

nine

nail

Pull here.

O is for ox

This oxen team will pull your youngsters through *O* obstacles.

Ox With A Box Poem

Gather together a box and some props to enhance this poem.

> This is the ox
> Who has a box.
> An ox with a box is he.
> Inside the box he has [some socks],
> [Some socks] for all to see!

Repeat the poem, substituting *some blocks, some rocks, a fox* (photo or illustration) *some clocks,* and other rhyming choices for the words in the last two lines.

Big *O* Bagel

Provide your youngsters with a variety of bakery bagels, minibagels, or bagels you bake in class using your favorite recipe. Slice each bagel in half and spread it with cream cheese. Slice pitted black olives to make little letter *O*s. Let each youngster decorate their big *O* bagel with little olive *O*s.

"Oh, Who Is On The Ox?"

This ox song fits quite well to the tune of "The Farmer In The Dell."

> Oh, who is on the ox?
> Oh, who is on the ox?
> High, ho, away we go!
> Oh, who is on the ox?
>
> The [cat] is on the ox.
> The [cat] is on the ox.
> [Meow, meow,] away we go!
> The [cat] is on the ox.

Repeat the verse for other animals and corresponding animal sounds that your students suggest.

Ox With A Box Booklet Page

Use the *O* booklet page on page 104 as directed for previous letters. Have each youngster draw a picture or glue on magazine pictures to fill the box. Write each child's dictation in the space provided to list and describe the contents of the box.

Big Ox Art

Create a big *O* bulletin board with the patterns on pages 105 and 106. Reproduce each pattern page on colored construction paper. Have each child cut out the pattern pieces and glue them together, then color in some facial features. Provide your students with a variety of materials to decorate their oxen such as *O*-shaped cereal, newspaper and magazine *O*s, letter *O* rubber stamps, and even old water faucet rubber washers! Have students select their materials and then glue them to their paper oxen. Post these awesome oxen on a bulletin board titled "*O* Is For Ox."

Ox Cart Foldout Book

Reproduce the patterns on pages 107 and 108 on white construction paper. Have your youngsters color the ox and cart pieces and cut them out. Have them cut out the two book pages and glue all four of the cut-out pieces together where indicated. Color the *O* picture pieces, cut them out, and glue each one to a box in the center of a cart section. Fold up the book accordion-style and fold it out to read it.

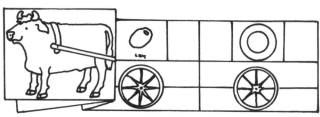

The Ox-Cart Man
by Donald Hall

• As you read the story, have your youngsters generate a list of the things that the family put in the ox cart to take to market, such as wool, a shawl, mittens, candles, etc. Have your students take turns drawing *O*s around the letter *O*s as they find them in the words.

• Ask your youngsters to focus on the ox in the story by describing its appearance and how it helped the farmer. Ask them to decide if the family might have treated the ox like a pet and what they might have named it. Have them search the winter barn illustration for signs of another ox and then discuss its relationship to the first ox.

• Enlarge the cart pattern on page 107 to provide a cart for each child on an 8 1/2" x 11" piece of paper. Have each youngster draw something from the story to color, cut out, and glue to the cart. Write the vocabulary word from the story under the cart.

More *O* Books

Paul Bunyan by Steven Kellogg
Paul Bunyan And Babe The Blue Ox by Jan Gleiter and Kathleen Thompson
Octopus Protests by Jacquelyn Reinach
Otter Rescue by Jill Bailey

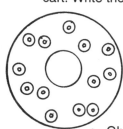

More Ox and *O* Activities

• Glue *O*-shaped cereal to a small paper plate after cutting out a circle from the center. Have each child hold up his finished *O* and say a word that begins with *O*.

• Fill a small jar with colored, fruit-flavored *O*-shaped cereal and have your students estimate how many are in the jar. Count together as a class to find the actual amount.

• Give each youngster a large section of newspaper and a bright colored felt pen. Have him color the centers of all the *O*s he finds on the sheet. Each student should count his *O*s and share the number with the class.

• Collect pictures of items that are *O* shaped. Share them with the children and discuss what the items are, where you would find them, and what you would do with them.

• Share with your students that oxen are very strong and are used to pull heavy loads in other parts of the world where there is less machinery. They usually work in pairs with a wooden piece between them called a yoke which keeps them walking and pulling together. Use two of the completed patterns on pages 105 and 106 and tie them together with a paper-created yoke.

• Serve super *O* treats of mini doughnuts or orange slices.

Ox

The ox has a box. In the box is a

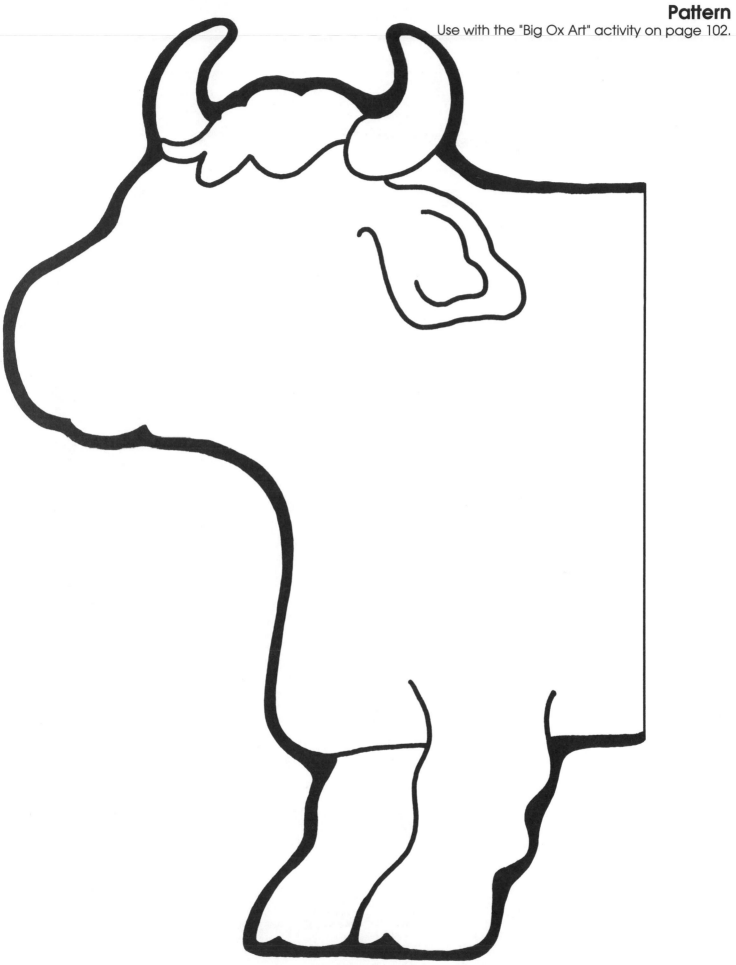

Pattern

Use with the "Big Ox Art" activity on page 102.

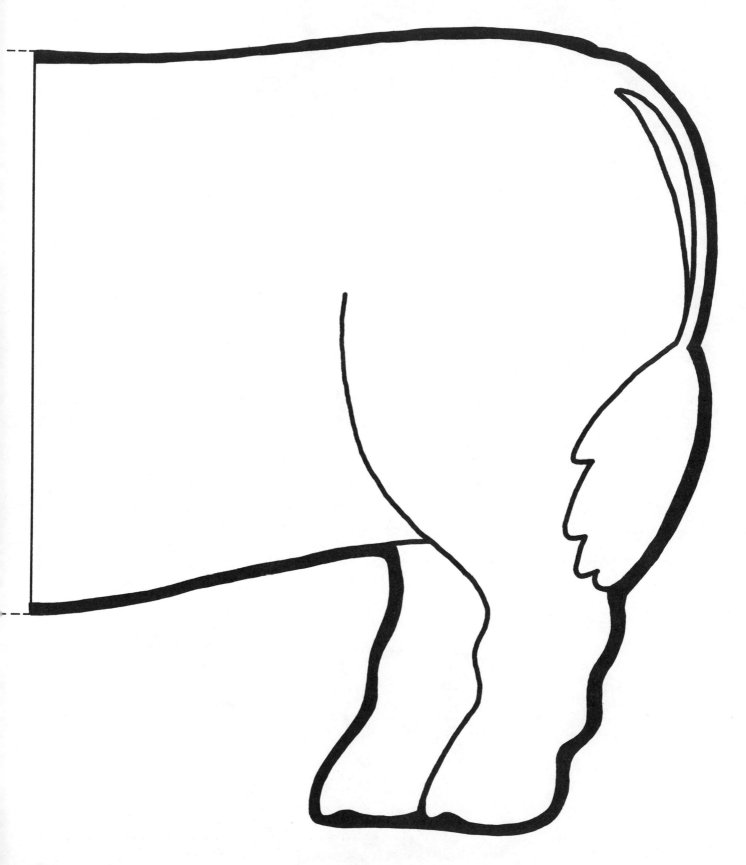

Patterns

Use with the "Ox Cart Foldout Book" activity on page 103.
Use the cart pattern with the third activity for *The Ox-Cart Man* on page 103.

O picture pieces

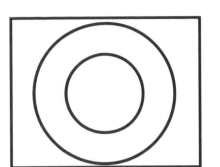

cart pattern

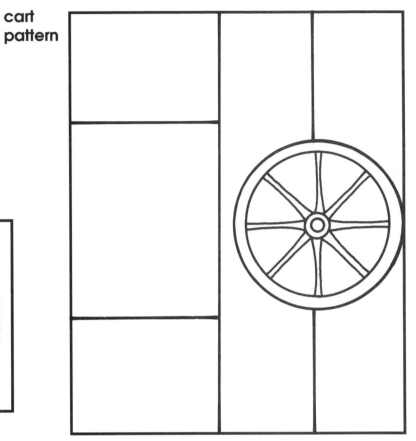

octopus

ostrich

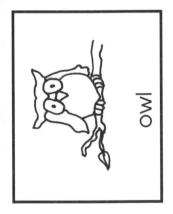

owl

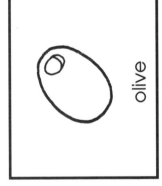

olive

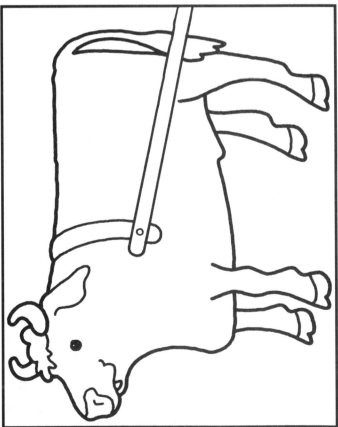

ox pattern

Foldout Book Pages Patterns

Use with the "Ox Cart Foldout Book" activity on page 103.

Glue to the ox.

Glue to the cart.

Glue to the other strip.

P is for pumpkin

Use pumpkin power to present the letter *P!*

"This Little Pumpkin" Poem

Have your youngsters create their own movements to accompany each line.

This little pumpkin was small and round.
This little pumpkin sat on the ground.
This little pumpkin was short and fat.
This little pumpkin wore a silly hat.
This little pumpkin had a grin so keen.
This little pumpkin said, "Happy Halloween!"

Accompany the poem with large student-painted pumpkin pictures, one picture for each verse in the poem.

Yummy Pumpkin Muffins

Mixing up these spicy pumpkin muffins will have your youngsters grinning like jack-o'-lanterns!

2 cups flour
2 tsp. baking powder
3/4 tsp. ground cinnamon
1/2 tsp. salt
1/2 tsp. ground ginger
1/4 tsp. ground cloves
1/3 cup butter or margarine, softened
1/2 cup packed brown sugar
2 eggs
1 cup cooked, mashed pumpkin (or canned pumpkin)
1/2 cup milk
1/4 cup honey
1 cup golden raisins

Preheat oven to 375 degrees. Prepare a 12-cup muffin tin. Set aside. Sift together dry ingredients, except brown sugar. Set aside. Beat butter and brown sugar together in a large bowl. Add eggs, pumpkin, milk, and honey. Beat until light and fluffy. Stir in dry ingredients until just combined. Do *not* over mix or beat! Stir in raisins. Divide batter evenly among muffin cups. Bake 25–30 minutes or until muffins are springy to the touch and brown on top.

"The Pumpkins Are Here"

Bring in the pumpkins with this song sung to the tune of "The Farmer In The Dell."

The pumpkins are here; the pumpkins are there.
The pumpkins, the pumpkins are everywhere.

The pumpkins are up; the pumpkins are down.
The pumpkins, the pumpkins are all around.

The pumpkins are in; the pumpkins are out.
The pumpkins, the pumpkins are all about.

The pumpkins are low; the pumpkins are high.
The pumpkins, the pumpkins all say, "Good-bye."

Pumpkin Booklet Page

Use the *P* booklet page on page 111 as directed for previous letters. Write each child's dictation in the space provided to complete the sentence starter. Have each child lightly color her pumpkin with an orange crayon.

Pumpkin People

Your youngsters will be pleased to make these perky paper people. Reproduce the shirt and pants patterns on page 112 on white construction paper. Reproduce the pumpkin head pattern on page 113 on orange construction paper. Color the shirt and pants, and add facial features to the head. Cut them out. Glue the shirt to the pants. Glue the head to the shirt. Have each child select a name that begins with the letter *P* for his pumpkin person. Use a wide felt-tip marker to write these names on the shirts of the pumpkin people.

Pumpkin Project

Reproduce the pumpkin project patterns on pages 113, 114, and 115 on orange construction paper. Cut out all of the pumpkin pieces (pages 114 and 115). Glue the cover bottom to the bottom of the backing piece, using a thin stream of glue where indicated to make a pocket. Staple the cover top to the top of the backing piece to cover the seed outlines. Cut out the pumpkin seed pieces and place them in the pocket for storage. To use the project, have your students look at the object pictured on each seed and say its name. Place a seed piece on a seed outline if the picture begins with the P sound.

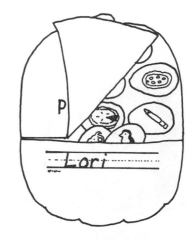

Pumpkin, Pumpkin
by Jeanne Titherington

- Write the following vocabulary words on large green construction-paper leaf cutouts:

  | pumpkin | plant | pick |
  | pumpkins | planted | picked |

  Post a pumpkin cutout on a board along with the title "Pumpkin, Pumpkin." Attach the labeled leaf cutouts around the pumpkin and add some green curling ribbon for vines.

- Have your students examine the seeds and seed packet on the book's title page. Ask them to propose different places that the seed packet could have come from.

- Have youngsters demonstrate how to plant a pumpkin seed. Have children take turns using a hoe and other props to "plant" a seed or a button in a sandy area, explaining the reasons for their actions as they progress through the steps.

More Pumpkin Prose

The Biggest Pumpkin Ever by Steven Kroll
Mousekin's Golden House by Edna Miller
The Vanishing Pumpkin by Tony Johnston

More Pumpkin and *P* Activities

- Display a large plastic pumpkin in the classroom and add items that begin with the letter *P* such as pins, pens, pencils, pipe, and paper. Encourage your students to bring in other items to put into the pumpkin that begin with *P* and share them with the class.

- Paint the letter *P* with purple and pink paint. Have children search through their crayons and find other *P* colors.

- Discuss with your youngsters where the seeds are found in a pumpkin. If possible, cut a fresh pumpkin and have the students take turns digging out the seeds. Explain that some people eat pumpkin seeds as a snack but they must be baked first. Wash the seeds, spread them on a cookie sheet, salt lightly, and bake at 350 degrees for 15 minutes or until light brown and crispy.

- Have each student plant pumpkin seeds in a paper cup. Divide a packet of pumpkin seeds so each student has 3-4 seeds. Poke two small holes with a pencil in the bottom of each paper cup. Fill each cup 1/2 full of soil and have the children push the seeds into the soil and cover them up. Set the paper cups in a large shallow container and water until moist.

- Serve a pile of peanuts (dry roasted) for a nutritious snack.

Pumpkin

Here is a pretty pumpkin.

It is

Patterns
Pumpkin Person
Use with the "Pumpkin People" activity on page 109.

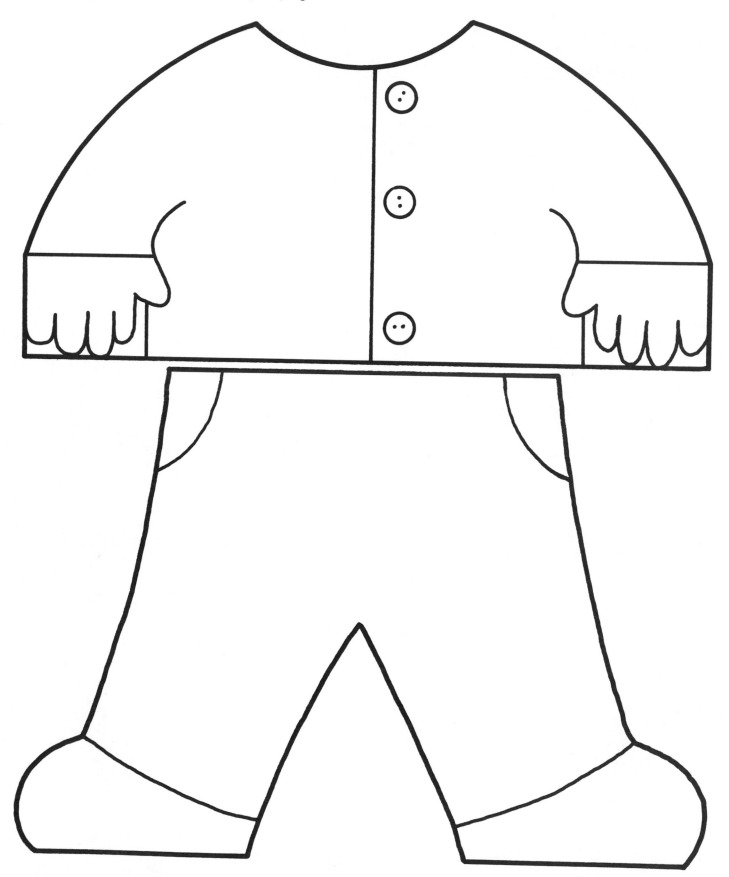

Pattern
Pumpkin Head
Use with the "Pumpkin People" activity on page 109.

Pattern
Backing Piece

Use with the "Pumpkin Project" activity on page 110.

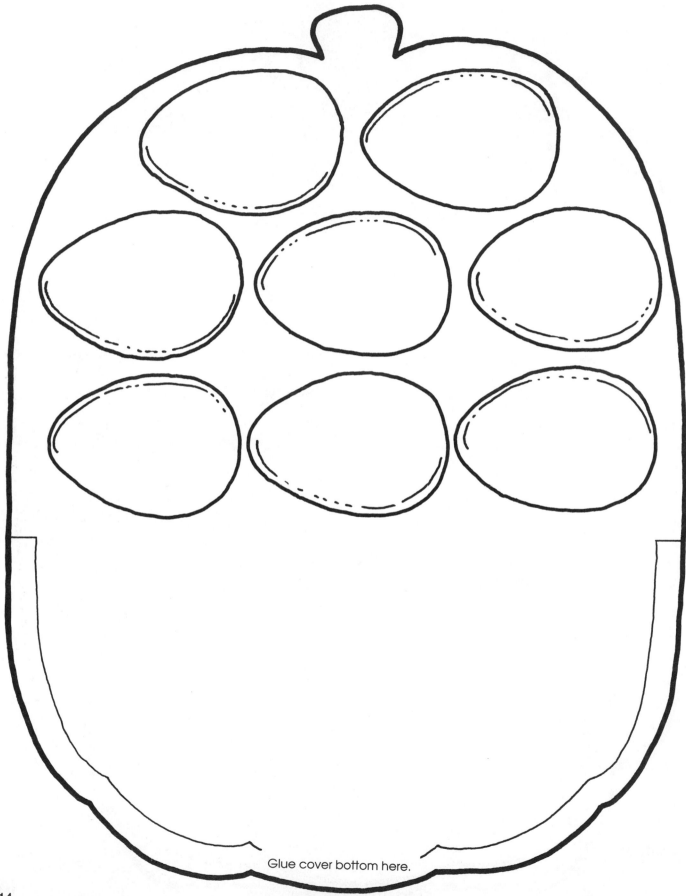

Glue cover bottom here.

cover top

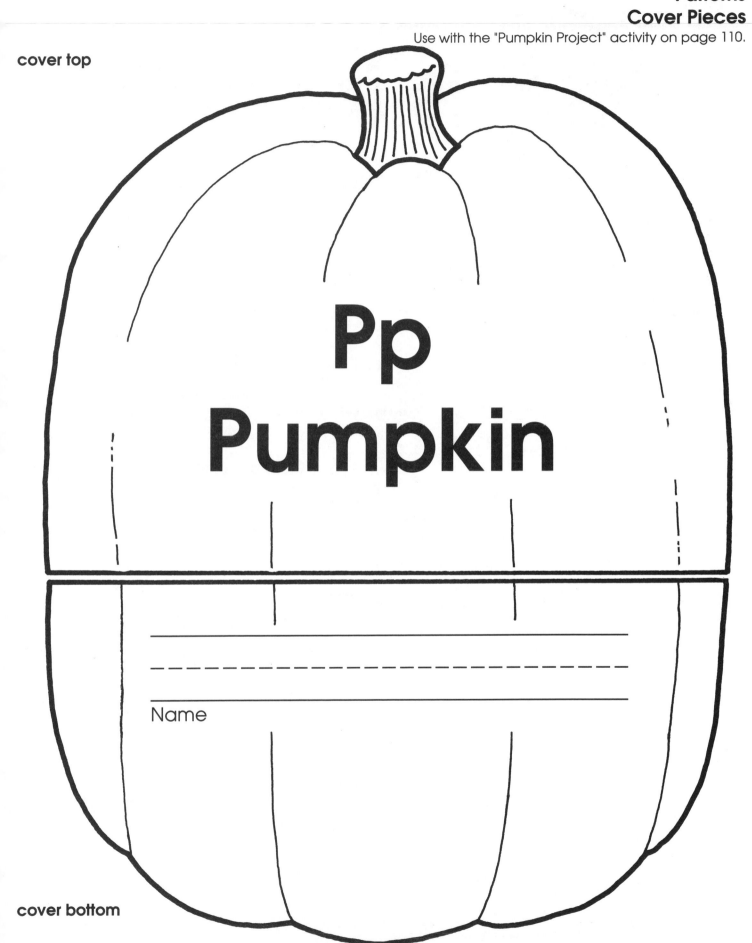

Pp
Pumpkin

Name

cover bottom

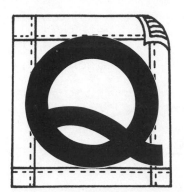

Q is for quilt

Wrap up some Q learning fun in a cozy letter quilt.

The Quilt Poem

Have your youngsters make up actions to accompany this poem.

Cut some squares of colored cloth.
Lay them side by side.
Sew the squares with strong, strong thread
Until the quilt is wide.

Fill the quilt with fluffy stuff.
Sew it all around.
Now your quilt is certainly
The nicest to be found.

Put the quilt upon your bed.
Tuck it in so tight.
It will keep you nice and warm
All through the cold, cold night.

"A Cozy Quilt For Me!"

Sing this short little song to the tune of "B-I-N-G-O!"

Here's a cozy little quilt,
As warm as it can be!
Q-U-I-L-T, Q-U-I-L-T, Q-U-I-L-T.
A cozy quilt for [me].

Have your students sit in a circle. Use a small doll quilt as a prop. As you sing the song each time, have a new child hold the quilt. Insert the quilt holder's name at the end of line four.

Quilt Booklet Page

Use the Q booklet page on page 118 as directed for previous letters. Have each child color each quilt square with a different color of crayon. Write each child's dictation in the space provided to describe her quilt's color and/or appearance.

Snack Cake Quilt

Bake a large sheet cake. Let it cool and frost with white frosting. Use squeeze-tube frosting with a narrow tip to divide the cake into square sections to resemble the squares of a quilt. Mark off one square per child, if possible. Provide a selection of cake toppings such as chopped nuts, raisins, and a variety of decorative candies. Let each student decorate one square of the quilt cake. Encourage each youngster to decorate his square differently from the other ones around his own.

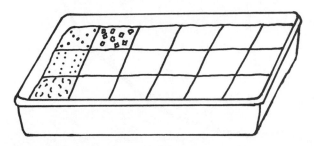

Classroom Quilt

Have your youngsters make this easy construction-paper quilt to brighten your classroom and warm your heart. Reproduce one quilt square (pattern on page 119) per child on white construction paper. Have each child color his quilt square's border with solid colors. Have him decorate the four corner triangles with crayon patterns such as dots, stripes, or stars. Use the central diamond shape for a student-drawn self-portrait. Cut out each square. Post all of the squares on a bulletin board to create a cozy class quilt. Alternately, use the pattern as a cover for student-made books.

A Queen's Quilt

Reproduce the patterns on pages 120, 121, and 122 on white construction paper. Ask your youngsters to color the large backing page with crayons, using a variety of colors to make it more quiltlike. Cut out the backing page along the bold outline. Have your students color and cut out all six minipages. Stack the pages with "A Queen's Quilt" title page on top. Center the stacked pages over the large *Q* on the backing page. Staple the pages to the backing page along the left side.

The Quilt Story
by Tony Johnston

- Abigail used her quilt for many different things. Have your youngsters list the things that Abigail used the quilt for. Ask them to add more of their own ideas in a similar list. Use the quilt square pattern on page 119 to inspire some creative writing. Have students use their own thoughts to finish this sentence: "I would use a quilt for…." Write their dictations in the center diamonds on the quilt squares. Color the rest of the squares.

- Let your youngsters tell you what critters "borrowed" Abigail's quilt when it was in the attic and what each critter used it for. Ask them to speculate why Abigail was not using the quilt.

- Ask your youngsters to think about the identity of the little girl in the second half of the story. Have them look for clues in the illustration: the portrait of Abigail, the similarities between Abigail's attic and the girl's attic, and so on. Have them look for similarities in how the quilt helped both girls.

Cozy Quilt Stories

The Canada Geese Quilt by Natalie Kinsey-Warnock
The Keeping Quilt by Patricia Polacco
The Patchwork Lady by Mary K. Whittington
The Quilt by Ann Jonas
Eight Hands Round: A Patchwork Alphabet by Ann Whitford Paul

More Quilt and Q Activities

- Photocopy, enlarge, and cut out quarter coin reproductions. Glue the large quarter coins to a large *Q* cut out of bulletin-board paper.

- Make a Venn diagram on the board listing the names of animals that are quick such as rabbits, mice, and chipmunks. In a second circle, list the names of animals that are quiet such as giraffes, rabbits, and turtles. Discuss the animals in the overlapping section that are both.

- Have the youngsters bring in remnant pieces of cloth from home. Cut the pieces into uniform square shapes and glue onto a piece of bulletin-board paper. When complete, attach the quilt to the bulletin board and add the title "Quiet Workers." Add students' names when they are caught working quietly.

- Reproduce the letter *Q* on 4" x 5" paper and have each student color and cut out the *Q*. Attach the paper *Q* to a Popsicle stick and encourage the children to hold them up when they feel it is too loud in the classroom and it needs to get quiet quickly.

- Explain to the children that some sentences tell things and some sentences ask things. Those asking sentences are called questions. Have your youngsters play a game by asking a question and calling on someone who knows the answer.

Quilt

The queen's quilt was made of many colors.

It was

Use with the "Classroom Quilt" activity on page 116 and the first activity for *The Quilt Story* on page 117.

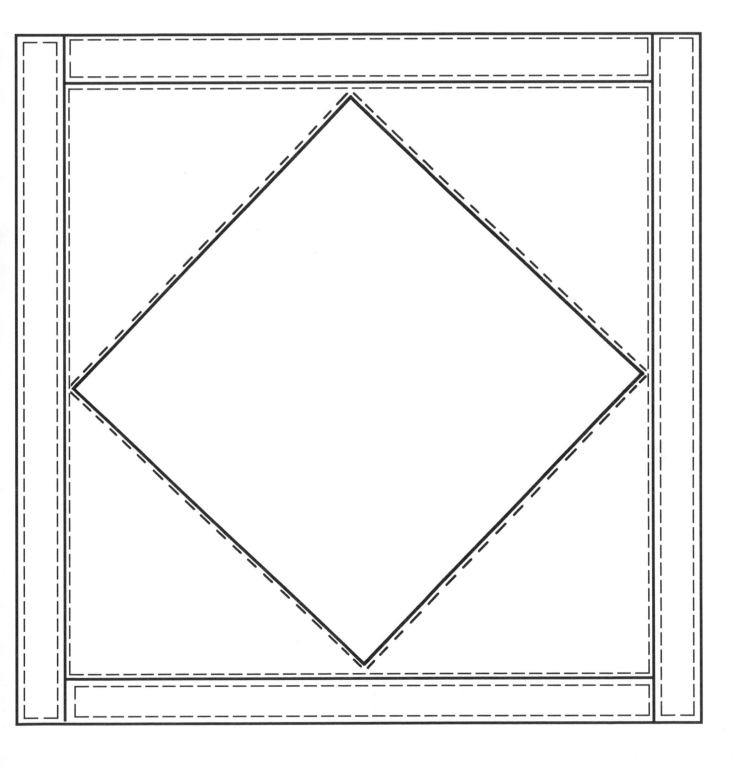

Pattern
Backing Page
Use with "A Queen's Quilt" activity on page 117.

A
Queen's
Quilt

quarter

question
mark

?

quail

quack

queen

R is for rabbit

Irresistible rabbits keep this *R* unit hopping along.

Run, Rabbit, Run

Run, rabbit, run
Till the day is done.
Run, rabbit, run
All day.

Race, rabbit, race
Till you find your place.
Race, rabbit, race
All day.

Rest, rabbit, rest
Till you feel your best.
Rest, rabbit, rest
All day!

Make simple rabbit puppets out of clean, used socks and felt scraps to accompany the poem. Cut ears, eyes, and a nose from felt. Sew or glue them to the sock puppet. Sew on thin yarn whiskers, if desired.

Silly Rabbit Salad

Even picky eaters will enjoy this naturally sweet salad! Use a small ice-cream scoop to scoop low-fat cottage cheese onto a small plate. Transform this humble, healthful dairy product into Silly Rabbit Salad by adding a red grape nose, thin celery slivers for whiskers, two banana slices for ears, and two raisin eyes.

"Rabbits Here And Rabbits There"

Sing this song to the tune of "Jack And Jill."

1. Rabbits here and rabbits there,
    Running all a-round.
    Rabbits in and rabbits out,
    Hopping up and down.

2. Rabbits sniff and rabbits twitch
    Their funny little noses.
    Rabbits hip and rabbits hop
    On furry little "toeses."

3. Rabbits wig and rabbits wag
    Their ears up in the air.
    Rabbits fluff and rabbits puff
    Their tails a-way back there!

Racing Rabbit Booklet Page

Use the *R* booklet page on page 125 as directed for previous letters. Have each child draw and color an object on the ground beneath the rabbit. Write each child's dictation in the space provided to complete the sentence starter.

Foldup Rabbit

Reproduce the patterns on pages 126 and 127 on white or pastel-colored construction paper. Cut out all of the pieces. Glue the large feet piece to the bottom of the body, placing the glue strip behind the body piece. Glue the two upper paws to the sides of the body, placing the glue strips behind the body. Glue the two ears to the top of the body piece as shown.

For an art activity, color the rabbit and add facial features cut from construction paper. For creative writing, add facial features only and write each student's dictation on the body section of the rabbit. The students can dictate a short story titled "Rabbit Runs." Fold all paw pieces to cover the body.

123

"Rabbit Reads About Things That Begin With *R*" Book

Make this fun little booklet to provide each youngster with a mini *R*-sound book. Duplicate the patterns on pages 128 and 129 on white construction paper. Cut out the backing piece along the outline. Have each student write his name on the byline. Cut out the picture pages and stack them with the *R* title page on top. Staple the picture pages to the backing piece along the right side.

Too Many Hopkins
by Tomie dePaola

• Mommy Hopkins organized her active family in order to get through spring planting. Have your youngsters list the chores from the story in their correct sequence. Let small groups of youngsters pantomime each chore.

• The Hopkins triplets and the four sets of twins were set apart by their sets of rhyming names. Have your youngsters brainstorm a list of new names that begin with *R*. Divide the list of rhyming sets of names into a list for the girls and one for the boys.

• Collect small garden tools and supplies to display in a small wheelbarrow along with easy-to-read vocabulary cards telling their names. Attach the word cards to the tools with yarn. Allow your youngsters time to examine the tools and read their names.

Really Good Rabbit Reads

Max's Chocolate Chicken by Rosemary Wells
Rabbit's Morning by Nancy Tafuri
Ten Little Rabbits by Virginia Grossman
To Rabbittown by April Halprin Wayland

More Rabbit and *R* Activities

• Cut graduated lengths of rope from one inch to one foot. Have youngsters arrange the ropes in a pyramid shape with the shortest at the top and the longest at the bottom.

• Color a large rainbow for a bulletin board. Cut out large paper raindrops and have each student print upper and lowercase *R*s on his raindrop. Pin up the students' raindrops on the bulletin board and title it "A Rainbow of Raindrops."

• Explain to the children that a rainbow is formed when sunlight shines through the rain. Use a prism on an overhead projector to show the colors of a rainbow. (Often the glass on the overhead will split the light and shine the spectrum on the wall.)

• Hang a piece of rope from the wall and attach all of the students' names that begin with *R*. Have each *R* student circle the *R* in his name with a red marker.

• Provide an *R* snack of mini ricecakes spread with raspberry jam. Top with raisins, if desired.

R   r

Rabbit

The rabbit raced.

He raced over a

Pattern
Use with the "Foldup Rabbit" activity on page 123.

body

126

ears

finished project

Rabbit runs to get carrots!

feet

Glue to back of rabbit bottom.
FOLD

paws

Glue to back of rabbit's side.

Glue to back of rabbit's side.

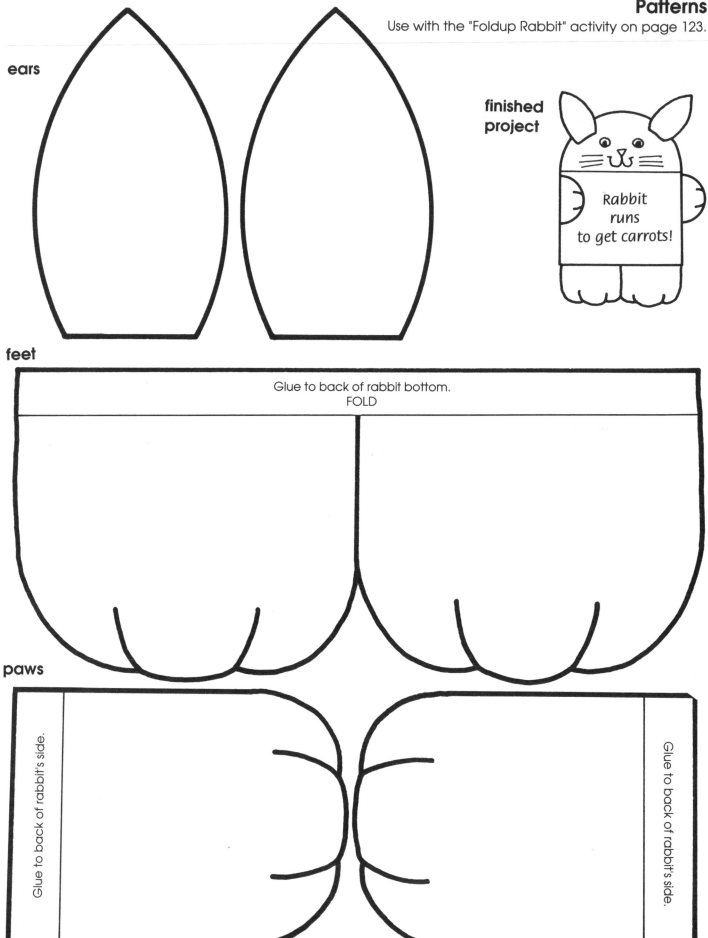

Use with the " Rabbit Reads About... Book" activity on page 124.

Rabbit Reads About

by

_____

Patterns
Title Page And Picture Page

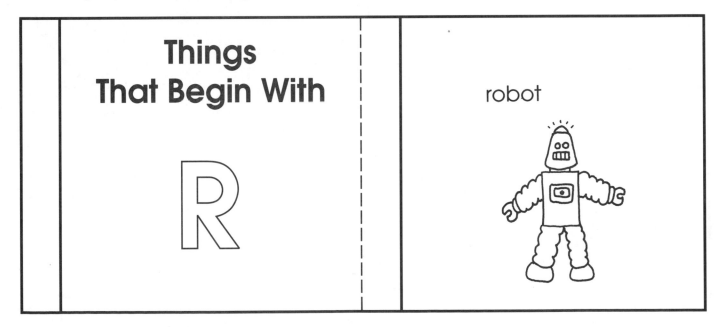

Things
That Begin With

R

robot

rope

rainbow

raccoon

rake

rocket

ring

 **is for sunflower**

Plant the *S* seed with some sunflower fun.

A Sunflower Grows

Have children use these actions to accompany this sunflower poem.

A sunflower starts
With a tiny seed.
(Crouch down small like a seed.)
Soil, sun, and water
Are what it needs.
(Pretend to pat soil around feet.)
A sunflower sprouts
From something small—
(Kneel with arms out.)
To something strong
And straight and tall.
(Stand tall, arms out.)

"Plant A Sunflower"

Sing this song to the tune of "Frère Jacques."

1. Plant a seed, plant a seed.
   Help it grow, help it grow.
   Cover it with soil, cover it with soil.
   Watch it grow, watch it grow.

2. Plant a seed, plant a seed.
   Help it grow, help it grow.
   Give it lots of sun, give it lots of sun.
   Watch it grow, watch it grow.

Repeat the verse, replacing the third and fourth lines with:

3. Give it water showers, give it water showers.
   Soon you'll have a sunflower, soon you'll have a sunflower.

A Sunflower Snack

Cut a circle from a slice of bread to make the center of your sunflower. Spread peanut butter on the bread and top it with shelled sunflower seeds. Arrange the bread on a plate along with corn chip "petals" and a celery stalk stem.

Super Sunflower Booklet Page

Use the *S* booklet page on page 132 as directed for previous letters. Have each child draw and color a large sunflower atop the stem. Write each child's dictation in the space provided above the picture of the girl to describe the sunflower's size.

Super-Sized Sunflower

Set your bulletin board abloom with this super-sized art activity. Provide each youngster with the patterns on pages 133 and 134 reproduced on yellow construction paper. Have them sponge-paint the flower center with brown paint. When the paint is dry, cut out the flower center. Cut out the flower petals and glue them around the circumference of the center. Glue whole sunflower seeds to the flower center. Display the sunflowers on a bulletin board highlighted by a smiling construction-paper sun.

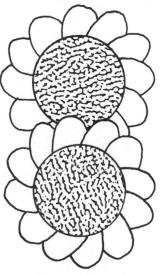

S Is For Sunflower

Make a fun matching game using the patterns on pages 135 and 136. Reproduce the "S Is For Sunflower" patterns on white construction paper. Cut out the triangle shape on each flower along the dotted lines. Have your youngsters color the flowers and cut out the rectangle along the bold lines. Punch a hole in the center of each wheel and in the center of each flower. Attach each wheel behind a flower with a brad. Have your students turn the wheels to match a picture to a word.

Wild Wild Sunflower Child Anna
by Nancy White Carlstrom

- Ask your students to decide who is telling the story about Anna and why the storyteller calls her "sunflower child." Have them list things that outdoor-loving Anna has in common with a sunflower.

- Have your students study the large sunflower on the first page of the story and the smaller sunflowers on the last two pages. Ask your students to tell you what characteristics make the two flower varieties alike and what makes them different.

- Anna is a child who loves nature and probably loves being called "sunflower child." Have each youngster choose something that he really loves. Help each child make up a nickname like Anna's that reinforces his special interest. Have each child draw a picture to illustrate his Anna-style nickname. Write his nickname on his picture page.

Sunflower Stories

And A Sunflower Grew by Aileen Fisher
Sunflower! by Martha McKeen Welch
Sunflowers by Cynthia Overbeck
Sunflowers by Kathleen Pohl

More Sunflower and S Activities

- Involve the children in a seed-sorting activity. Bring in several kinds of seeds mixed together in a large jar. Divide the children into groups of four and challenge each group to sort the seeds into categories. Allow each group to sort the seeds according to its own criteria. Have each group share its method.

- Cut a large paper *S* from bulletin-board paper and hang it on the wall. Give each student two lengths of string and two pieces of tape. Allow each student to attach his string to the *S* and call it the "Silly String *S*."

- Have your students use sunflower seeds as counters during math lessons. Fill paper cups 1/2 full of soil and allow each student to plant his counters. Be sure to poke a small hole in the bottom of the cup with a pencil for drainage. Keep the cups moist.

- Have a *silly sock* day and allow the children to wear the silliest sock combination they can imagine. Wear your silliest socks also.

- Make *S* soup by displaying a large pot in the room that can be filled with items that begin with *S*. Begin the soup by adding a stone and challenge the children to bring more *S* ingredients.

- Bring a large bottle of soda and share it with your class.

- Present your students with the award badge on page 136. Highlight each child's badge with a photocopy of his school picture.

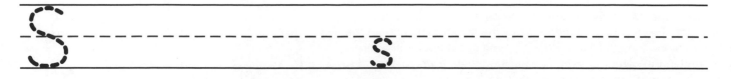

Sunflower

My sunflower is as big as a

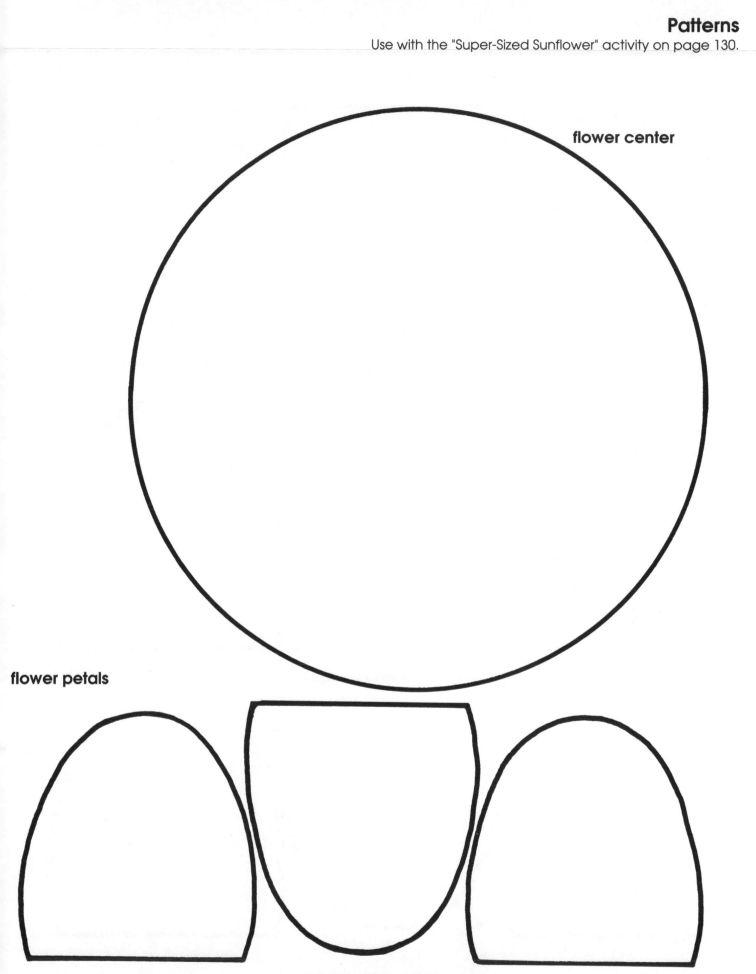

flower center

flower petals

Patterns
Flower Petals
Use with the "Super-Sized Sunflower" activity on page 130.

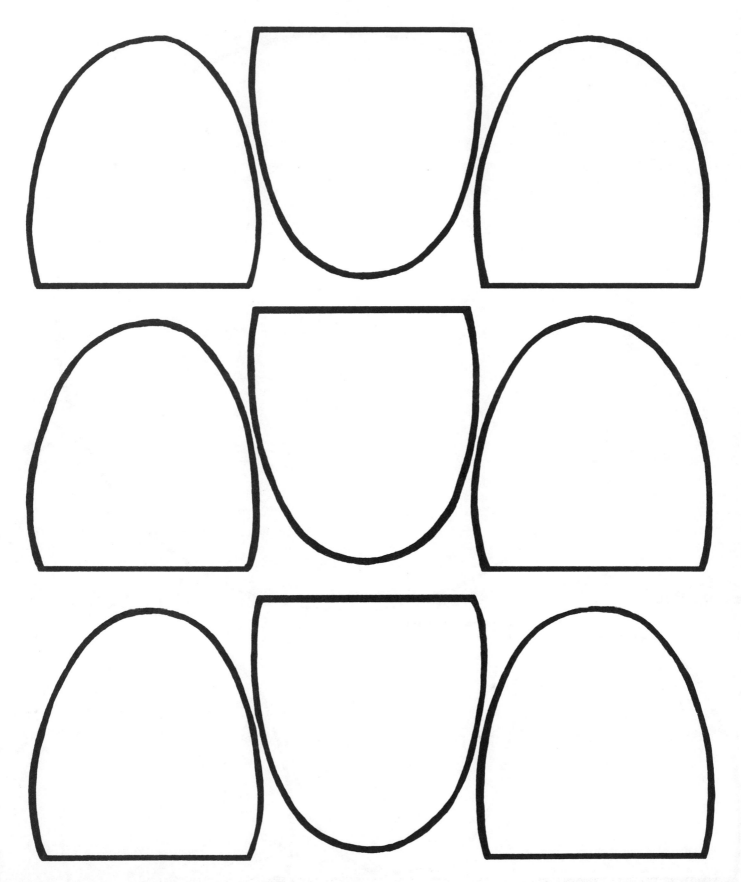

s is for sunflower.

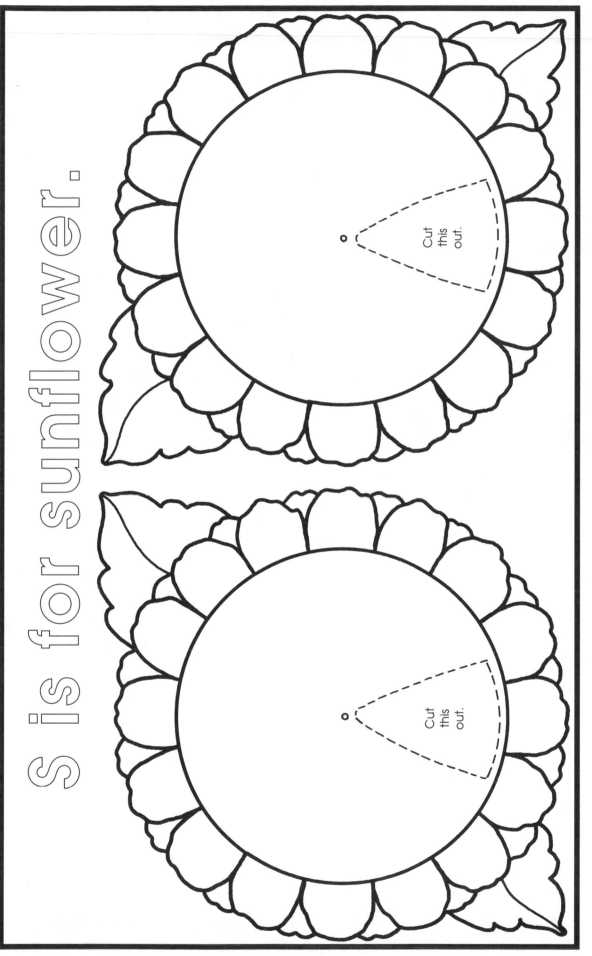

Cut this out.

Cut this out.

Patterns
Use the word and picture circles with the "*S* Is For Sunflower" activity on page 131.

Use the word and picture circles with the "*S* Is For Sunflower" activity on page 131.

Award Badge
Use with the last "More Sunflower and S Activities" on page 131.

Use with the last "More Sunflower and S Activities" on page 131.

word circle

seed
sack
sock
seal
sun
soap

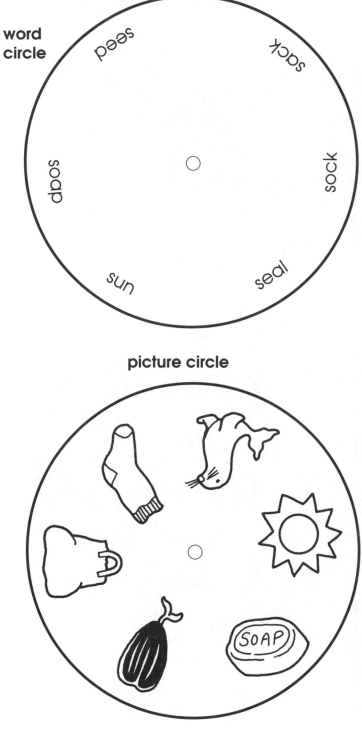

picture circle

SOAP

S

is for

Super

Student

T is for turtle

Turtles may be slow, but they'll suit your youngsters to a *T.*

Turtle Action Poem

Your youngsters will have fun performing these actions.

1. A turtle's fond
   Of any pond
   Where it can take a swim. *(Pretend to swim.)*

2. Turtles hide
   Away inside
   Their shells where it is dim. *(Cover eyes.)*

3. Turtles spy
   A bug or fly
   And snap it up to eat. *(Clap hands.)*

4. Turtles go
   So very slow
   On pokey turtle feet. *(Walk in place slowly.)*

Turtle Treats

Choose your favorite recipe for sugar cookies. Tint the cookie dough with green food coloring. Have each youngster roll a walnut-sized ball for a turtle body. Place the ball on a cookie sheet and press it down with the tines of a floured fork. Press down with the fork again at right angles to form cross-hatching for the turtle's shell. Roll a smaller ball for a head; press the head firmly into one end of the cookie "shell." Press two almond slices into each side of the cookie shell for legs. Poke one thin almond sliver into the end opposite the head for the tail. Bake at the temperature called for in your recipe. Watch to be sure that the almonds don't burn.

Turtle Song

Sing this song to the tune of "Row, Row, Row Your Boat."

1. Turtles, turtles go.
   Turtles go so slow!
   Turtles walk and poke along.
   Turtles go so slow!

2. Turtles, turtles swim.
   Turtles swim so well.
   Turtles splish and splash along.
   Turtles swim so well.

3. Turtles, turtles hide;
   Turtles in their shells.
   Turtles hide away inside;
   Turtles in their shells.

Turtle Booklet Page

Use the *T* booklet page on page 139 as directed for previous letters. Have each child draw a picture of something that he imagines the turtle could carry on its back. Write each child's dictation in the space provided to describe the turtle's cargo!

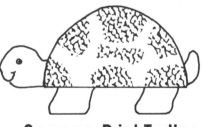

Sponge-Print Turtles

Help your youngsters make these terrific turtles for a bulletin-board display. Reproduce the body, head, and tail patterns on pages 140 and 143 on light green construction paper. Have your students color these pieces with crayons, adding an eye and a mouth. Sponge-print a design on the turtle's shell with dark green paint. Use a variety of sponge shapes for printing. Let the turtle shell dry and cut it out. Cut out the head and tail. Glue the head and tail to the body, positioning the glue strips behind the body. Cover a bulletin board with brown paper for the ground and blue paper for the water. Post the turtles and title the board "Turtle Territory."

"*T* Is For Turtle" Tachistoscope

Reproduce the patterns on pages 141, 142, and 143 on white construction paper. Have your youngsters color the turtle cover and backing pieces, then cut them out along the bold outlines. Cut out the large *T* and glue it to the space on the turtle cover. Slit along the dotted lines on the turtle backing. Staple the cover atop the backing piece along the left side. Help your students color, cut out, and glue the two sections of the picture strip together; then thread the picture strip through the slits on the turtle backing page.

I Wish I Could Fly
by Ron Maris

- As you read the story, have your youngsters make a list of the things that the turtle *can't* do. Have your students describe the things about the turtle's body that make it impossible to do these things. Have your youngsters list some words to describe how a turtle *can* move.

- Have your youngsters brainstorm a list of turtle names beginning with *T.* Have each youngster decide which name is her favorite. Graph your youngsters' choices on large chart paper or on a graph on the blackboard.

- Let your students use their favorite turtle names to inspire some creative writing about an imaginary turtle pet. Have them write about something their turtles can do. Mask the slit marks on a copy of the turtle pattern on page 142 and reproduce it on green paper. Write each child's story on a turtle.

More Turtle Stories

The Foolish Tortoise And The Greedy Python
  by Richard Buckley
Rosebud by Ed Emberley
The Smallest Turtle by Lynley Dodd
Turtle And Tortoise by Vincent Serventy

More Turtle and *T* Activities

- Set up a small dome-type tent in a corner of your classroom and allow your students to use it in pairs for short periods of "Talking Time."

- Bring in a teapot. Write words that begin with *T* on cards and have your students choose one from the teapot to pantomime for the class to quess. The student who quesses correctly gets to choose the next card.

- Help the children recognize items that come in groups of ten such as fingers, toes, dollars (ten dollar bill), and pennies (dime). Make other groups by binding ten sticks with a rubber band.

- Fill a jar with taffy and have your children estimate how many pieces are in the jar. Count the pieces together as a class and write the numeral that stands for the number of pieces. Have each child count out the same number of tokens. When they have the same number counted out, they earn a piece of taffy for a treat.

- Explain to the children that turtles are a kind of animal called reptiles. They are cold-blooded which means that inside of their body is the same temperature as it is outside around them. If it is cold outside, they are cold inside. Help the children name other reptiles such as snakes, lizards, and alligators.

- Have your students ask if they could wear one of dad's old ties to school for *Tie Day.*

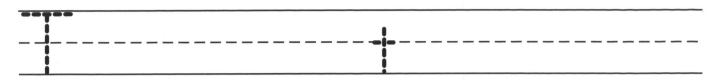

Turtle

The turtle carried something on its back.

It was a

Pattern

Use with the "Sponge-Print Turtles" activity on page 137.

turtle body

Patterns

Use with the " *T* Is For Turtle' Tachistoscope" activity on page 138.

turtle cover

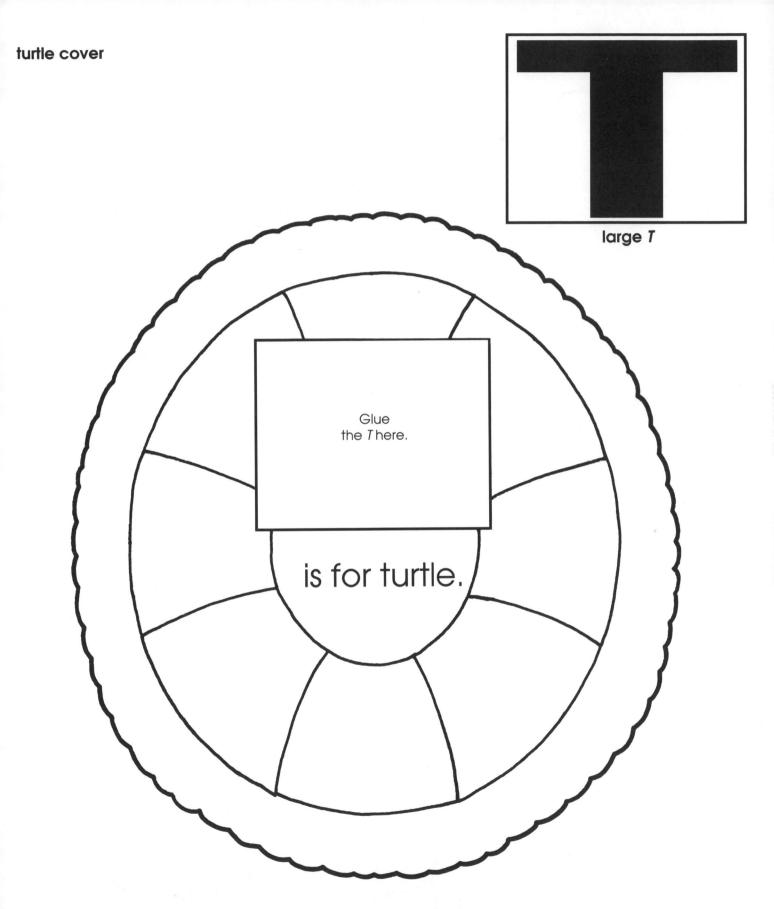

large *T*

Glue
the *T* here.

is for turtle.

Pattern
Turtle Backing

Use with the " '*T* Is For Turtle' Tachistoscope" activity and the third *I Wish I Could Fly* activity on page 138.

Patterns

Use with the " 'T Is For Turtle' Tachistoscope" activity on page 138.

Use with the "Sponge-Print Turtles" activity on page 137.

picture strips

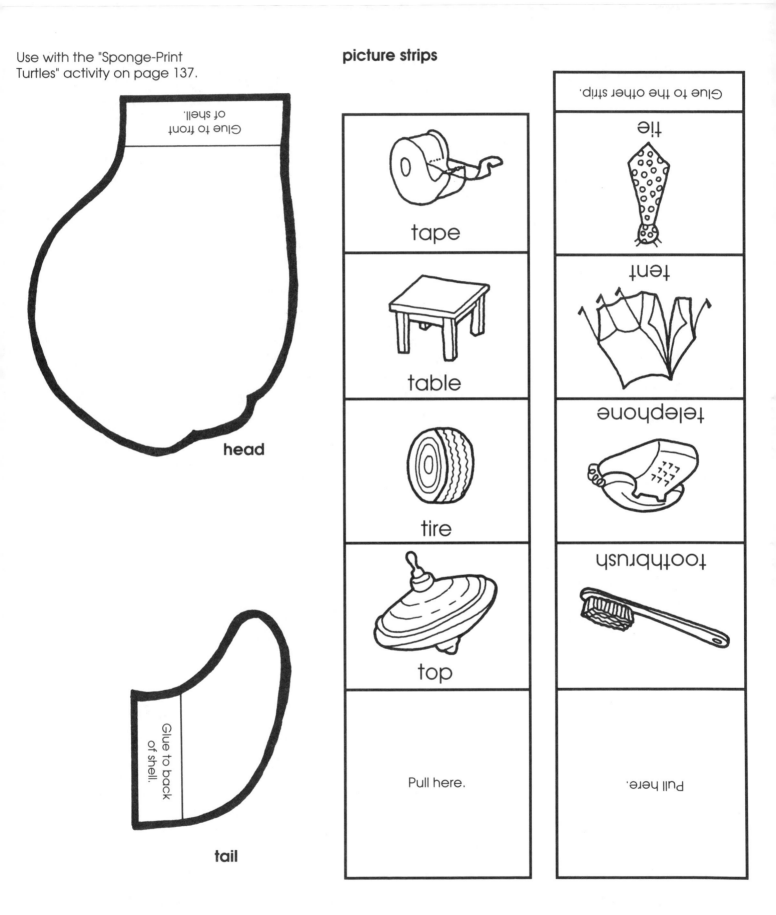

Glue to front of shell.

head

Glue to back of shell.

tail

tape

table

tire

top

Pull here.

Glue to the other strip.

tie

tent

telephone

toothbrush

Pull here.

U is for umbrella

Open an umbrella full of letter *U* doings.

Umbrella Poem

Use the construction-paper umbrellas from the "Ultimate Umbrellas" activity on this page as props to accompany this poem.

Umbrellas go up
When the rain falls down,
When the rain falls down on me.
Umbrellas go up
When the weather's wet
To keep the rain off me!

Umbrellas go up
When the sun shines down
On a hot day by the sea.
Umbrellas go up
When the weather's hot
To keep the sun off me!

Umbrella Song

Sing to the tune of "I'm A Little Teapot."

Here's my new umbrella.
Wide and high.
It keeps me cozy, warm, and dry.
If the rain starts falling from the sky
Just open me up and you'll stay dry!

Umbrella Booklet Page

Use the *U* booklet page on page 146 as directed for previous letters. Have each youngster draw something or someone underneath the beach umbrella. Write each child's dictation within the space provided to complete the sentence starter.

Orangey Umbrellas

Slice oranges into 1/4-inch-thick round slices. Cut each round slice in half to form a half-round umbrella shape. Place each orange umbrella on a small plate or napkin. Let each child choose an umbrella handle garnish from a selection of thin-sliced cheese, pretzel sticks, thin celery sticks, or thin apple slices.

Ultimate Umbrellas

Use the patterns on pages 147 and 148 to create unique umbrellas for a bulletin-board display or to accompany the "Umbrella Poem" activity on this page. Trace the umbrella top on folded tagboard; then cut it out to make a tracer. Trace around the umbrella-top tracer on white construction paper. Have students dribble tempera paint thinned with water onto their umbrellas and quickly blow the dribbled paint, using drinking straws, to create a spattered rain pattern. Let these dry. Have your youngsters color their handle and letter patterns, then cut out all of the project pieces. Glue the handle and letters to each umbrella top. Write each child's name on her handle.

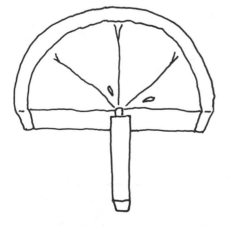

Short *U* Umbrellas

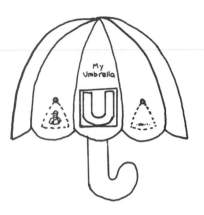

Set up some umbrella learning fun with the patterns on pages 149 and 150. Reproduce the patterns on white construction paper. Cut out the triangle shapes on the umbrella top along the dotted lines. Have your youngsters color all of their pattern pieces and cut them out. Punch holes in the umbrella top and the wheels where indicated. Attach each wheel to the umbrella with a brad. Glue the *U* and the handle to the umbrella. Have your students turn the wheels to match each picture to a word.

Umbrella
by Taro Yashima

- Momo loved her rainy-day birthday presents. Have your youngsters speculate on who gave the little girl her very own rain gear. Ask them to decide why she got an umbrella and boots rather than a doll or other toys.

- Momo was very creative with her ideas for the need to use her umbrella even though it wasn't raining. Ask your youngsters to think of some different ways to use an umbrella. Have each student dictate a short story titled "How To Use An Umbrella." Write each child's story on a construction-paper umbrella shape.

- Have your youngsters think about the sound that rain makes when it bounces off an umbrella. Have them make up sound effect words for bouncing raindrops. Let each child hold a large umbrella over his head; then sprinkle the umbrella with raindrops from a hose!

Some Umbrella Stories

Mr. Digby's Bad Day by Jerry Smath and Valerie Smath
Sally Sky Diver by Polly Noakes
The Umbrella Day by Nancy Evans Cooney
Umbrella Parade by Kathy Feczko

More Umbrella and *U* Activities

- Cut a three-dimensional *U* from a large sponge and introduce your children to the word under. Explain that this is your *under* sponge and you will place it under a new object each morning for them to discover when they arrive at school.

- Have some fun introducing the prefix *un*. Bring in a zipper and zip it up asking the children what we call this. Then unzip it and ask what we call it. Explain to the children that putting the prefix *un* in front of a word makes it mean the opposite such as zip/unzip, knot/unknot, and tie/untie. Work together to list other *un* words.

- Introduce students to synonyms for umbrella such as parasol and bumpershoot. A parasol was originally used to shade ladies from the sun but evolved into the waterproof version we have today. Help students brainstorm new synonyms for umbrella such as a *rainyday* or a *dropper stopper*.

- Write on raindrop-shaped cards the names of items that might go *up* and items you might find *under*. Hang a small open umbrella from the ceiling and attach these cards to the outside perimeter with string.

- Set up a large beach umbrella and place small pillows or carpet pieces underneath. Let students take turns using this special area for a quiet reading center. Post a sign stating "Shh! We Are Under The Umbrella!"

- Bake an upside-down cake (pineapple) and share it with your students for a super *U* snack. Have the children try to draw a picture or write their name upside down.

Umbrella

There was something under the umbrella.

It was

umbrella top

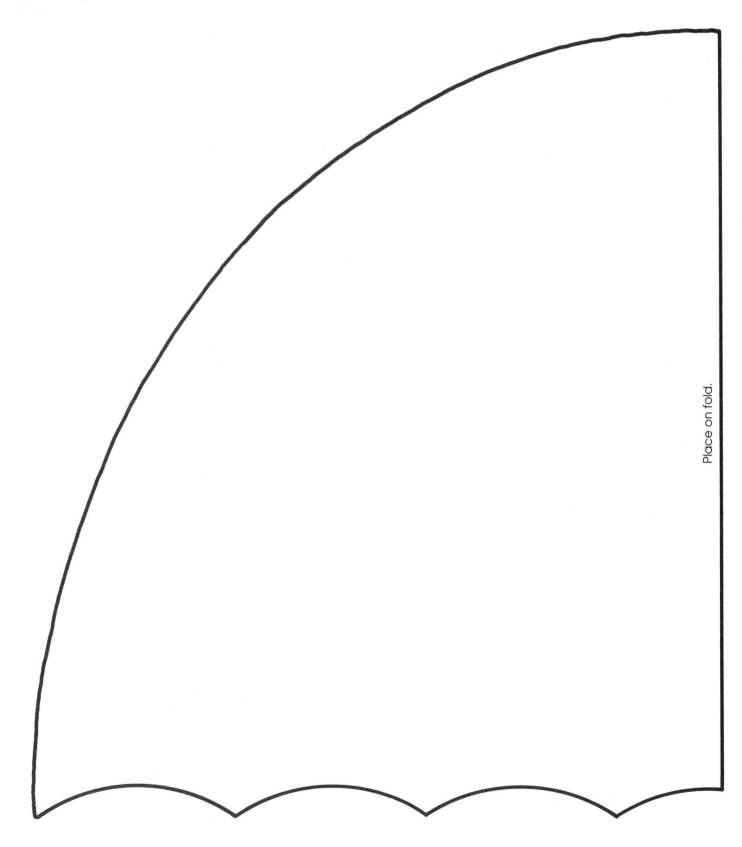

Place on fold.

Patterns

Use with the "Ultimate Umbrellas" activity on page 144.

umbrella handle

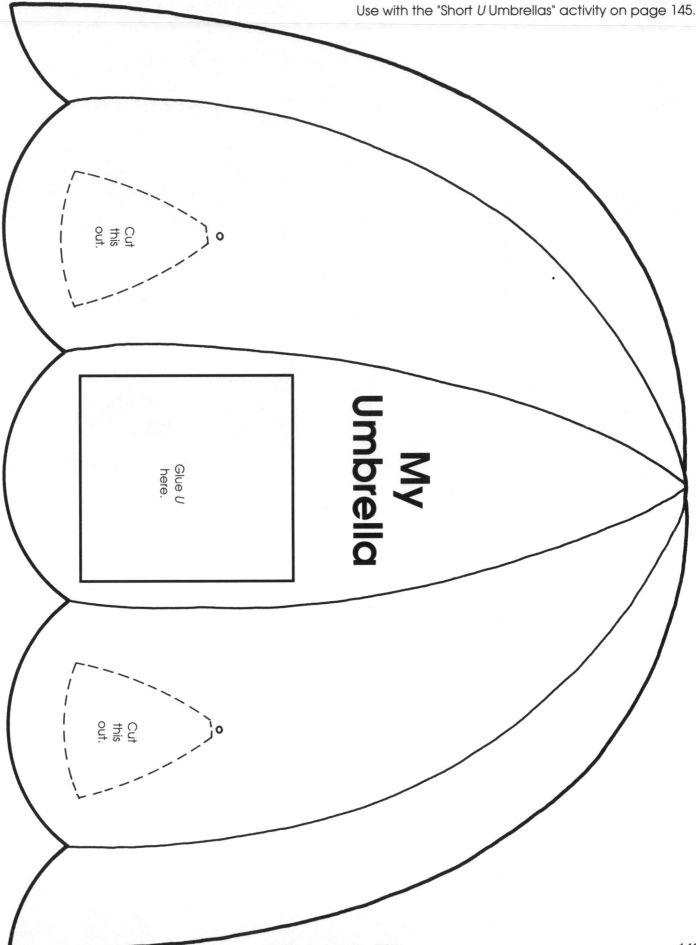

My
Umbrella

Glue *U*
here.

Cut
this
out.

Cut
this
out.

Patterns

Use with the "Short *U* Umbrellas" activity on page 145.

U pattern

umbrella
handle

picture wheel

word wheel

untied

under

upstairs

umpire

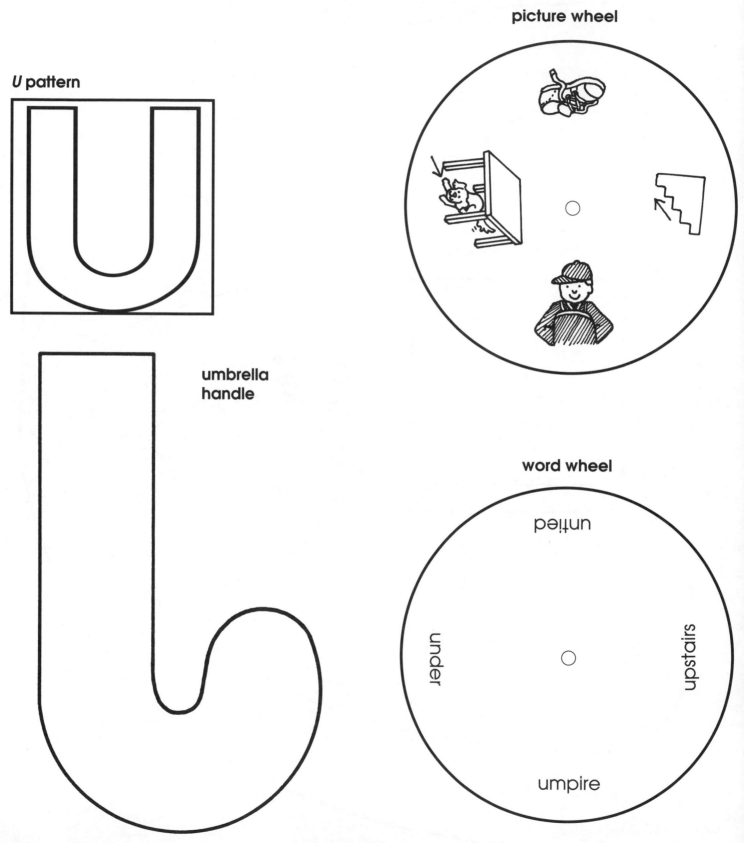

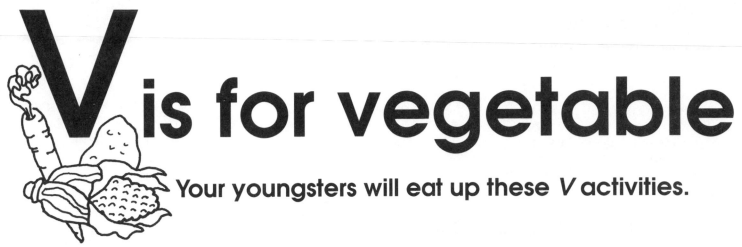

V is for vegetable

Your youngsters will eat up these *V* activities.

Vegetable Poem

Have your youngsters draw and color or sponge-paint large pictures of the vegetables in the poem to use as props.

Cabbage and broccoli, squash and peas.
Vegetables, vegetables, if you please!

Radish and cauliflower, beans and corn.
Vegetables, vegetables, cold or warm.

Lettuce and yams and carrots too.
Vegetables are so good for you!

Vegetable Munchies

Cut a variety of raw vegetables—including carrots, celery, and zucchini—into thin sticks. Add small, tender, whole, raw green beans and snow peas. Have each of your youngsters choose some of these vegetables to arrange into a *V* shape on a plate or napkin. Provide youngsters with a favorite dip to accompany their veggies. Serve these raw vegetables with small cups of your youngsters' favorite vegetable soup.

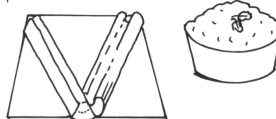

Vegetable Soup Song

Sing to the tune of "Baa, Baa, Black Sheep."

Buy some vegetables at the store.
Corn and peas and beans and more.
Wash the vegetables in the sink,
Let's make vegetable soup for lunch.
We love vegetable soup a bunch!

Put the vegetables in a pot.
Cook with broth until they're hot.
Use a bowl and big spoon too.
Vegetable soup is good for you!
Let's make vegetable soup for lunch.
We love vegetable soup a bunch!

Vegetable Booklet Page

Use the *V* booklet page on page 153 as directed for previous letters. Have each youngster color the vegetable pictures, then draw a large picture of her favorite vegetable in the space provided. Write each child's dictation within the space provided to describe her favorite vegetable.

Vegetable Vests

Students will enjoy creating some very vivid self-portraits using the patterns on page 154. Reproduce this page on white construction paper. Have your students color their vests and vegetable pictures and cut them out. Let each student glue the letter *V* and the pictures to the vest. Provide each child with a six-inch-diameter paper plate. Have him color the plate to create a portrait of his own face, then glue on yarn or construction-paper hair. Glue the paper-plate face to the vest where indicated. Post the projects on a bulletin board titled "Our Very Vivid Veggie Vests."

Vegetable Bag Project

Reproduce the bag, card, and pocket patterns on pages 155, 156, and 157 on white construction paper. Have your youngsters color and cut out the veggie bag front and back, the card pocket, and the picture cards. Glue or staple the card pocket to the bag back where indicated. Staple the bag front to the bag back along the left side. Place the picture cards in the card pocket for storage. Have a student select a picture card, say its name, and place it on one of the boxes on the bag back. For distractor cards, add extra cards programmed with pictures that begin with other letters if desired.

Growing Vegetable Soup
by Lois Ehlert

- Have your youngsters list the vegetables in the story. Have each student choose her favorite vegetable from the list, then draw it on an 8" x 8" square of paper. Tape each youngster's picture to the wall to form a graph that will show your youngsters' most popular vegetables. Discuss the resulting graph.

- Ask your youngsters to review the sequence of tasks from the story. Have each youngster tell you which task he would enjoy doing the most. Have youngsters work in small groups to illustrate the tasks. Display the groups' illustrations in sequence. Have children use them to retell the story.

- Assign each youngster a vegetable to bring to class. Display the vegetables and ask your students to name each one. Have students tell you descriptive words to describe each vegetable. Let them guess what each vegetable will look like on the inside. Use the vegetables to make a delicious pot of vegetable soup. Use the recipe at the end of the story as a guide. As you cut up the vegetables, let children describe what they actually look like inside.

Vivid Vegetable Stories

Grandpa's Garden Lunch by Judith Caseley
Moose In The Garden by Nancy White Carlstrom
The Trouble With Grandad by Babette Cole
Vegetable Garden by Douglas Florian
Vegetables by Susan Wake

More Vegetable And *V* Activities

- Bring in several packets of vegetable seeds and display the seeds next to the packet picture. Have your children hypothesize if large vegetables have large seeds and small vegetables have small seeds. You can expand this activity to compare color of seeds to vegetable color and shape of seed to vegetable shape. Have students glue a seed from each packet to a piece of construction paper and draw the vegetable next to it.

- Have each student bring in a canned vegetable. Make a display of the different kinds of vegetables and then donate the canned food to a local food bank.

- Make a vest for each student by cutting the corners off a paper bag, slitting the bag up the front, and cutting out the neck. Allow each student to decorate his vest with upper- and lowercase *V* and drawings of different vegetables.

- Invite a local musician to bring his violin or viola to play for the children.

- Have each student draw a vegetable valentine such as "I've *Bean* Thinking About You."

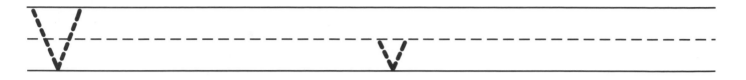

Vegetables

Here are some very good vegetables.

I like to eat

Patterns
Use with the "Vegetable Vests" activity on page 151.

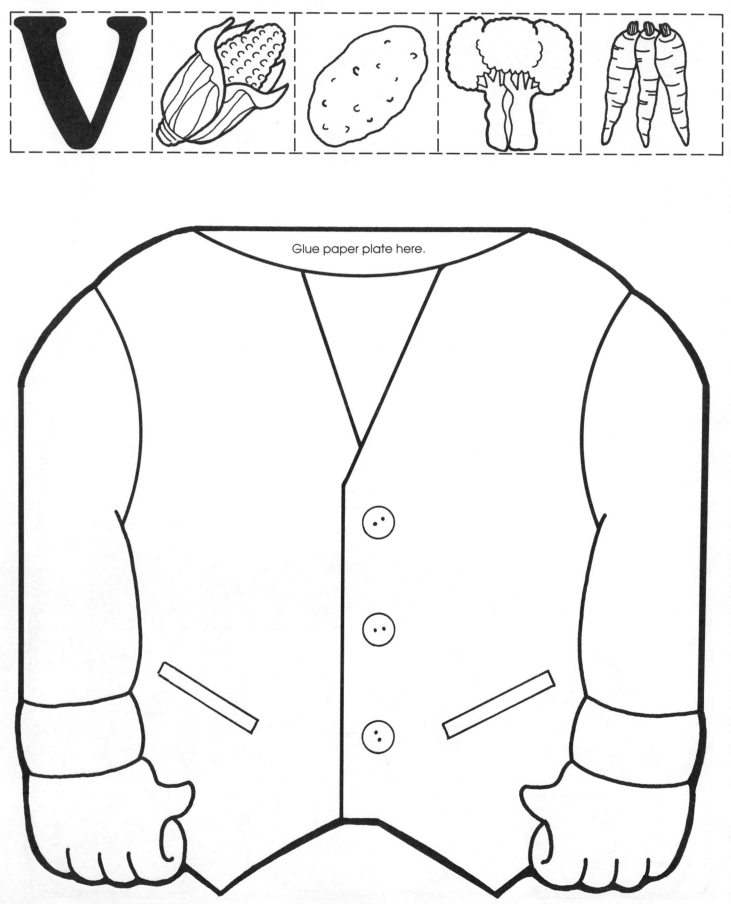

Glue paper plate here.

veggie bag
front

V

is for
vegetables.

Pattern

Use with the "Vegetable Bag Project" activity on page 152.

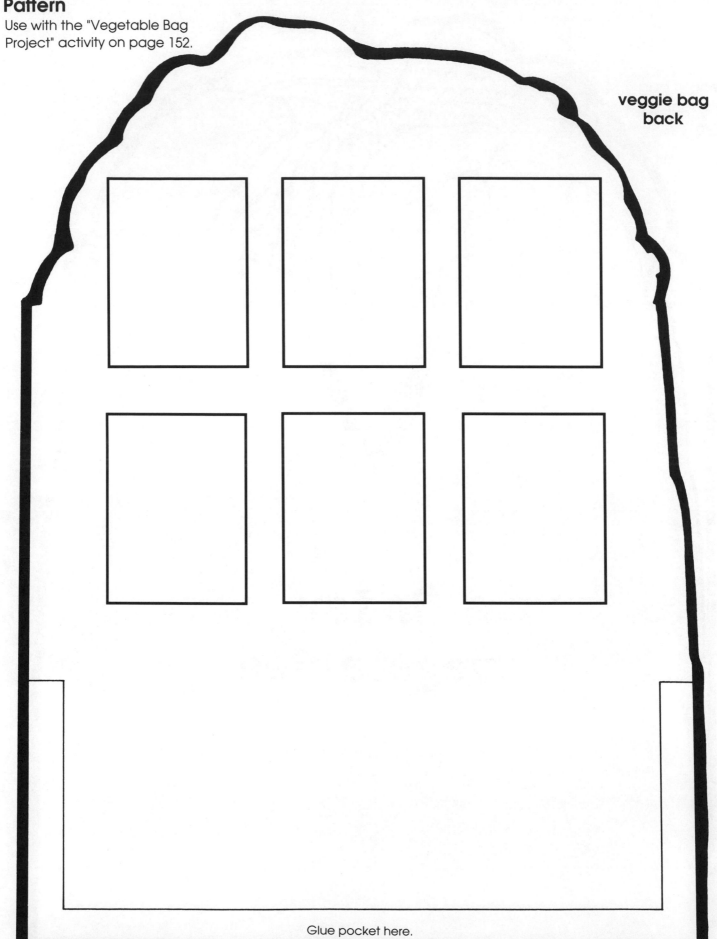

veggie bag back

Glue pocket here.

Use with the "Vegetable Bag Project" activity on page 152.

picture cards

vest

vase

violin

vulture

van

valentine

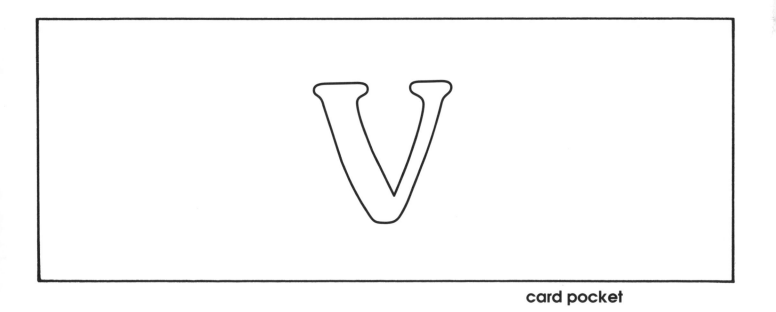

V

card pocket

W is for whale

Watch as whales inspire lots of *W* learning.

Whale Poem

This little poem will teach your youngsters a lot about whales.

A whale is not as small as us.
   (Shake head and finger.)
Most whales are bigger than a bus!
   (Stretch arms out wide.)
A whale is not like a fish in the sea.
   (Shake head and finger.)
A whale breathes air like you and me.
   (Take a deep breath.)
A whale can't walk upon the ground.
   (Shake head and finger.)
A whale must swim to get around.
   (Make swimming motions.)
A whale is a mammal just like me.
   (Nod head; point to self.)
But its home is in the deep blue sea.
   (Make wave motions with hands.)

Whale Cookies

Reduce the whale shape on page 163 and trace a very simple whale shape on cardboard. Cut out the cardboard whale to make a tracer. Prepare your favorite rolled cookie dough recipe. Roll out the dough. Place the whale tracer on the dough and cut around it with a knife to make a whale-shaped cookie. Bake one cookie for each child as directed in your recipe. When the cookies are cool, let each child frost his cookie with blue frosting. Have each child decorate his frosted cookie with a raisin eye and a short length of black shoestring licorice for a mouth.

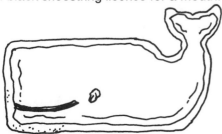

"Deep Down In The Sea"

Sing this simple song to the tune of "Row, Row, Row Your Boat."

Deep down in the sea
Lives a little whale.
She can swim and splash about
With her little tail.

Deep down in the sea
Lives a mama whale.
She can swim and splash about
With her great big tail.

Deep down in the sea
Lives a daddy whale.
He can swim and splash about
With his giant tail.

Whale Booklet Page

Use the *W* booklet page on page 160 as directed for previous letters. Have each youngster draw a picture of something that begins with *W* in the space provided at the bottom of the page. Write each child's dictation in the space above the whale to complete the sentence starter.

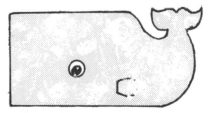

Sponge-Painted Whales

Create a sea full of lively whales to decorate a bulletin-board ocean. Reproduce the whale patterns on pages 161 and 162. Use thinned gray tempera paint to sponge-paint the whale front, tail, and flipper. When dry, sponge-paint the whale front, tail, and flipper with white paint (on top of the first paint layer) to create a mottled effect. Let them dry. Cut out the three painted pieces and glue them together where indicated. Color, cut out, and glue the eye to the whale. Display the whales on a blue-backed bulletin board titled "Wonderful Whales."

Whale Foldout Book

This little word book will make a whale of a splash with your youngsters. Reproduce the whale and picture card patterns on page 163 on light-blue construction paper. Reproduce the foldout pages on page 164 on white construction paper. Cut out the whale pieces, the picture cards, and the foldout pages. Glue the pages to the whale front and back where indicated. Have your youngsters glue each picture to its matching page. Fold the book up accordion-style.

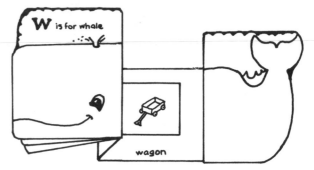

I Wonder If I'll See A Whale
by Frances Ward Weller

- Use colored chalk to write some of the *W* vocabulary words from the story on the board such as *whale, wonder, wharf, watch, wait, water, winter, warm, wheel,* and *wave.* Have your youngsters say each word with you to hear the *W* sound. Let various youngsters circle the *W*s with white chalk.

- Ask your youngsters why it is so hard for the people on the ship to see a whale. List students' ideas on a chalkboard or on chart paper. Have your youngsters discuss what things might help them spot a whale.

- The story tells us what the little girl thinks about the wonderful whales. Have each student pretend to be a whale. Ask youngsters to tell you how they feel as a *whale* seeing the boat and the people.

Whale Tales

Baby Beluga by Raffi
Humphrey: The Lost Whale by Wendy Tokuda and Richard Hall
John Tabor's Ride by Edward C. Day
The Whales' Song by Dyan Sheldon

Worm Farm

More Whale and *W* Activities

- Although whales do not make noise through their mouth, they do use their blow hole to produce sound. Have your students experience this sound by using a simple balloon. Blow up a balloon and hold it tight in your fingers. Explain that whales hold in air much like this balloon and they can let it escape as they please. Sometimes they let it out slowly by opening the blow hole just a little. Stretch open the top of the balloon and let the children hear the squeak of escaping air. Play a recording of whale sounds if available.

- Cut out a large wiggly-worm shape from bulletin-board paper and hang it from the wall. Have students think of words that begin with *W* and write them on the worm.

- Start a classroom worm farm. Buy a cup of earth worms at a bait shop and pour them into a clear plastic shoebox lined with two inches of top soil. Have the children look at the worms with a magnifying glass.

- Make waffle faces as a snack. Toast round mini waffles in a toaster oven, top with syrup, and have your students add raisins for eyes, nose, and mouth.

- Wear a funny wig to create *W* excitement. Declare a wig day and have the students bring wigs from home to model. Bring your camera for this one!

Whale

The whale looked underwater.

She saw a

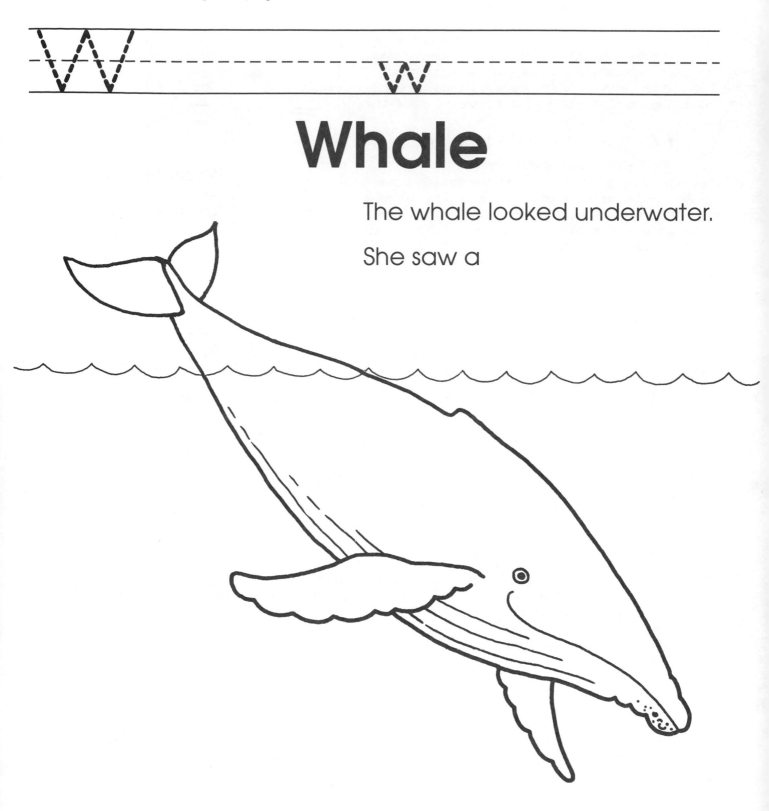

whale front

Glue
eye
here.

Patterns

Use with the "Sponge-Painted Whales" activity on page 158.

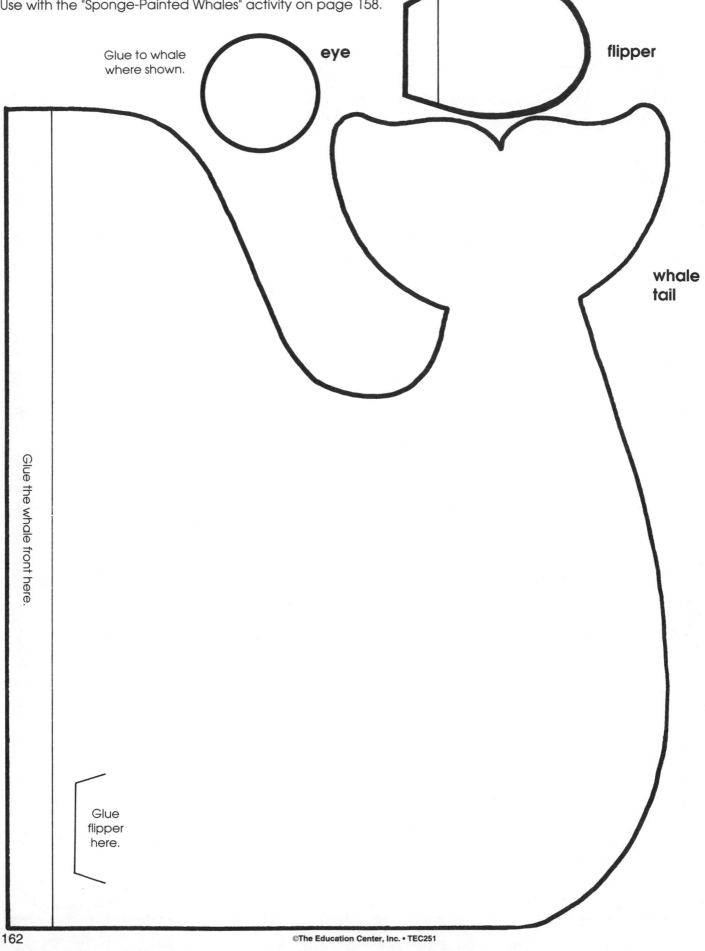

Glue to whale where shown.

eye

flipper

Glue the whale front here.

Glue flipper here.

whale tail

picture cards

whale front and back pieces
Use these with "Whale Cookies" on page 158 also.

W
is for whale.

Patterns
Foldout Book Pages
Use with the "Whale Foldout Book" activity on page 158.

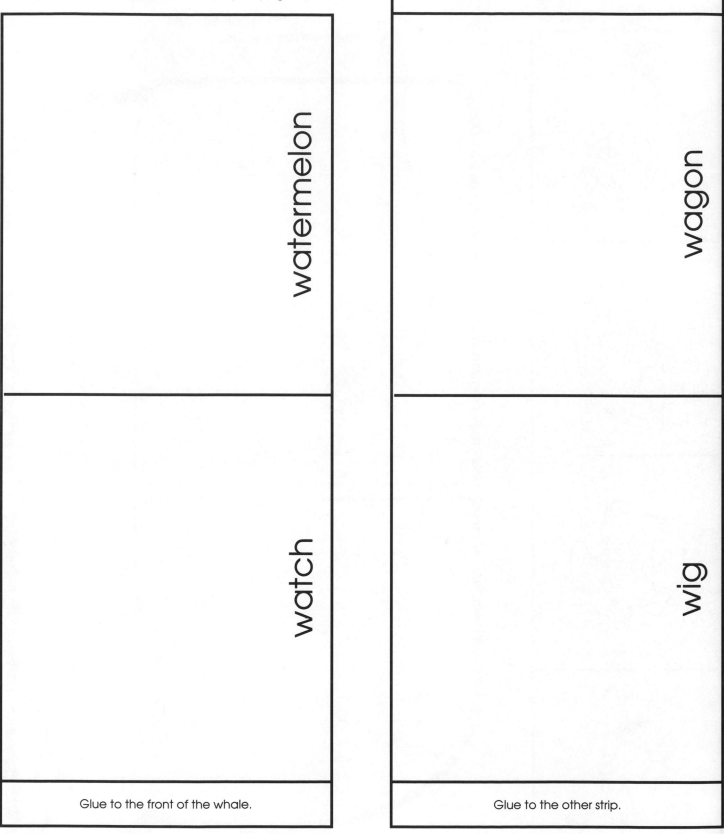

Glue to the back of the whale.

watermelon

wagon

watch

wig

Glue to the front of the whale.

Glue to the other strip.

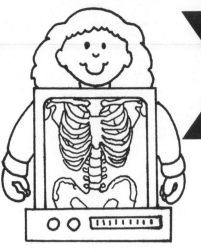

X is for X ray

X marks the spot where learning is fun.

X-ray Poem

Have your youngsters come up with pairs of rhyming words to extend the verses of the poem.

X-ray means "to see inside."
What if you had X-ray eyes?

Could you see inside a [rock]?
Could you see inside a [block]?

Could you see inside a [car]?
Could you see inside a [star]?

An X-ray Recipe

Make a large pan of Jell-O Jigglers™ from your youngsters' favorite flavor gelatin. Add cut-up fruit to the mixture while it is still liquid; then chill until firm. Cut the gelatin into *X* shapes, one per child. Students will be able to see inside their very own gelatin *X* just like an X ray!

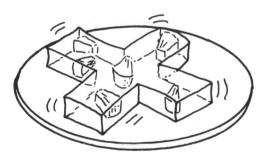

X-ray Booklet Page

Use the *X* booklet page on page 167 as directed for previous letters. Have each youngster draw something on the X-ray machine to show what might be inside the body. Write each child's dictation to complete the sentence starter.

"The Broken Arm"

Have students act out each verse of the poem.

1. One day I went out biking,
   But somehow I fell down.
   My poor arm hurt so very much
   My mom took me to town.

2. She took me to the doctor
   And the doctor said to me,
   "We'll give your arm an X ray
   To see what we can see."

3. The X ray took a picture
   To show the bone inside.
   The bone inside was broken!
   I very nearly cried!

4. The doctor said she'd fix me up
   So I'd be good as new.
   She wrapped my arm up in a cast
   And then her work was through.

5. My arm will soon be better.
   Then once again I'll ride.
   I'm very glad the X ray
   Could see my arm inside!

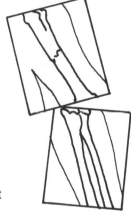

Activity Ideas For "The Broken Arm" Poem

- Survey your youngsters to find out if anyone has ever broken a bone. Have each youngster tell about his experience.

- After reading the poem aloud, have your youngsters list the sequence of steps in treating the break: from getting the X ray to putting on the cast. Ask a local X-ray lab for old X-ray pictures of broken bones to show your students.

- Use a large scarf to tie a simple sling around a youngster's arm. Have her wear the sling for a short length of time to see what it is like to have an arm out of commission.

X-ray Eyes

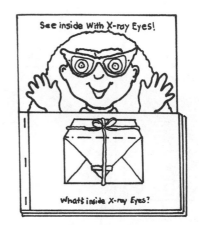

Students can imagine that they have X-ray vision as they construct and read this simple book. Reproduce pages 168, 169, 170, and 171 on white construction paper. Have each youngster color a large *X* on the lower half of the backing piece, then cut out the piece around the bold outline. Cut out the remaining six half-pages for each book and staple them in order to the lower left side of the backing piece where indicated. To make the book more of a surprise for your students, have an adult preassemble the books. Let students turn the pages and read along with you, guessing what's inside each package. Help them write the correct words on pages two, four, and six. Have students color their books.

An "X-tra" Large *X*

Make one very large *X* from tagboard for each child. Provide a variety of textured materials such as sandpaper, cotton balls, Styrofoam packing materials, foil, etc. Have each youngster select one material to glue onto her *X,* covering as much of the *X* as possible. When the *X* art is dry, ask each child to hold up and describe her *X.* Have her say, "I have an extra [adjective] *X.*" Your youngsters can insert adjectives such as *rough, soft, bumpy,* or *shiny.*

More X-ray and *X* Activities

- Call your local hospital, veterinarian, or X-ray facility and request X-ray "mistakes." Often, they will give teachers X-ray film they are not able to use.

- Have your students glue toothpicks to black construction paper in capital *X* shapes. They can break the toothpick in two for the lowercase *X.* Display their papers on a bulletin board titled "*X* Is *X*-Citing."

- Make a large simple map of your classroom and hang it on the wall. Hide a large sponge *X* somewhere in the room and mark the spot with a removable *X* on the map. Challenge your students to find the *X* by using the map. Before school each morning, choose a student to hide the *X* and change the map accordingly. Have that child choose a classmate to find the *X.*

- Provide your students with a slice of refrigerated cookie dough and a piece of wax paper. Have them divide the dough in half, roll both pieces into short snakes, and make an X with the dough. Place them on baking parchment paper and write each student's name next to his cookie. Bake as directed on the package and serve as a snack.

X X

X ray

The doctor took an X ray of Xavier.

He saw

The X-TRA Special X-RAY Machine

1 2 3 4 5 6 7 8 9 10

See Inside With X-ray Eyes!

Staple pages here.

is for X ray.

1

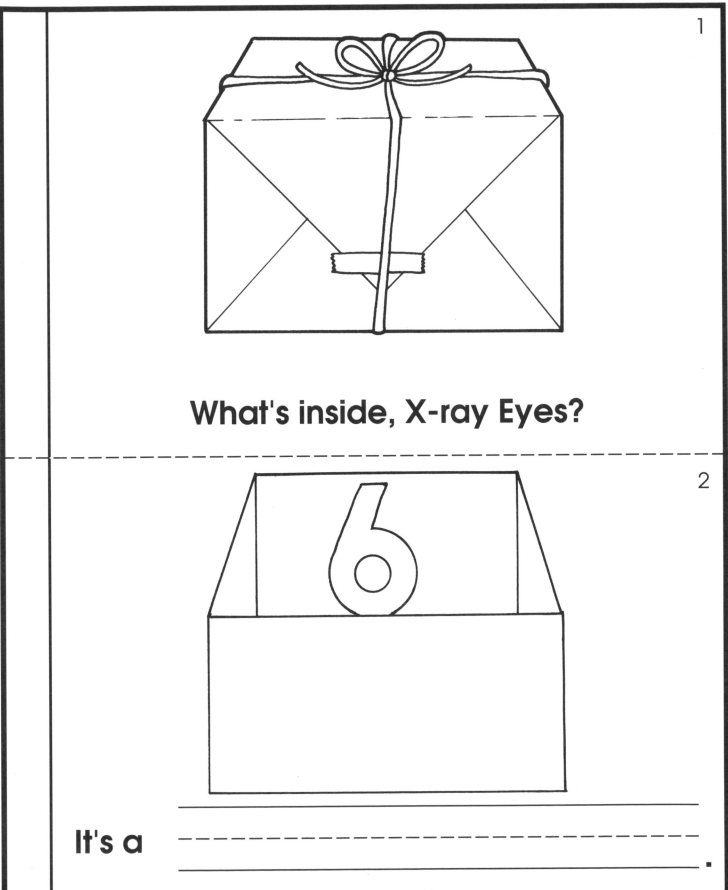

What's inside, X-ray Eyes?

2

It's a _____

3

What's inside, X-ray Eyes?

4

It's a _____

5

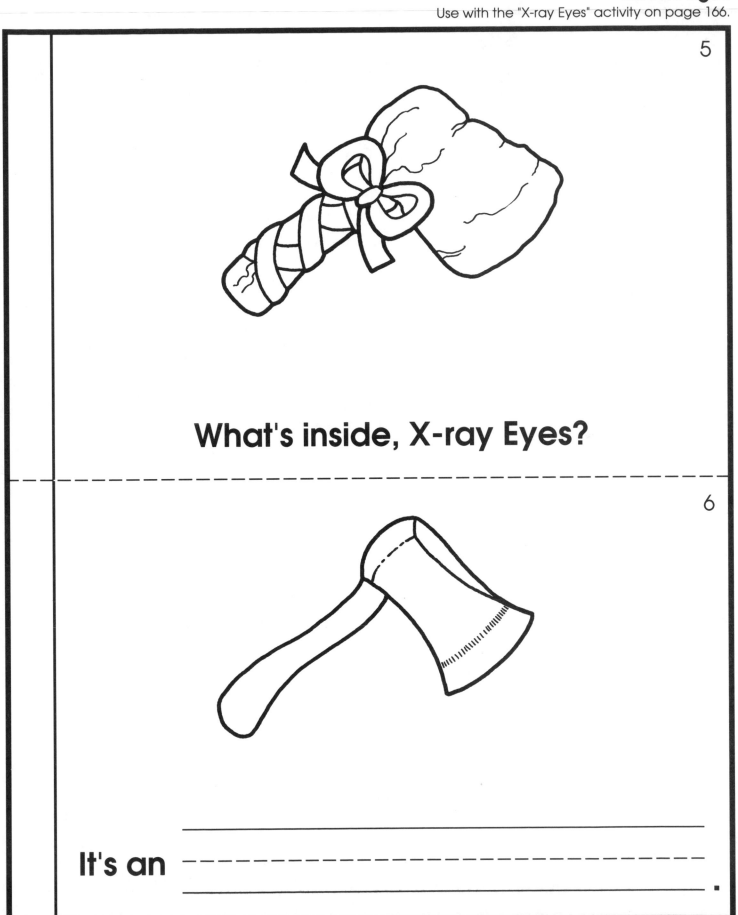

What's inside, X-ray Eyes?

6

It's an _____

Y is for yarn

One and all will have a ball with these *Y* activities.

Yarn Poem

It's fun to pass around a big ball of yarn as you sit in a circle to recite this poem.

What do you need
    (Point to head; then pretend to put on a hat.)
To make a warm hat?
Knit soft yarn to make a hat.

What do you need
    (Point to hands; then pretend to put on mittens.)
To make warm mittens?
Knit soft yarn to make some mittens.

What do you need
    (Point to neck; then pretend to put on a scarf.)
To make a warm scarf?
Knit soft yarn to make a scarf.

Silly "Yarn" Spaghetti

Serve some colorful but silly spaghetti for a snack. Cook spaghetti in water to which you've added food coloring, cooking it for the length of time directed on the package. Drain the cooked spaghetti and put it in a large bowl. Use very large knitting needles to serve a small amount of spaghetti to each child. Let students—just this once—use their fingers to eat their pasta "yarn"!

"Y-A-R-N"

This little song is sung to the tune of "A Bicycle Built For Two."

Y-A-R-N; use it to make a hat.
Y-A-R-N; use it to play with a cat.
Use yarn to knit up some mittens,
Warm yarn as soft as kittens.
Use yarn that's soft
And yarn that's blue
Just to knit something nice for you!

Yarn Booklet Page

Use the *Y* booklet page on page 174 as directed for previous letters. Have each youngster color the balls of yarn with his favorite colors. Write down each child's dictation describing what he might like to make out of the yarn such as a hat, mittens, or a sweater.

Shaggy Yellow Yaks

Hang these shaggy yaks from the ceiling or display them on a bulletin board. Reproduce the yak pattern on page 175 on light-colored construction paper. Have each youngster color in eyes on his yak's face; then cut on the bold outline. Have him glue five-inch lengths of yarn to the yak's back using thin and thick types of yarn for an interesting textured look. Display these critters with the heading "Shaggy Yellow Yaks!"

Follow The Yellow Yarn

Your youngsters will enjoy embellishing the pages of this booklet with circular, curvy, and zigzag designs in yellow yarn. Reproduce the patterns on pages 176, 177, and 178 on white construction paper. Have the youngsters cut the pages apart. Cut lengths of yellow yarn for students to glue to each page. Help each child apply a thin line of white glue along the dotted line on each page. Then have each child glue yarn to the dotted lines. Show children how to hold the yarn in place until the glue begins to set. When the glue has dried, staple the pages together in order along the left side.

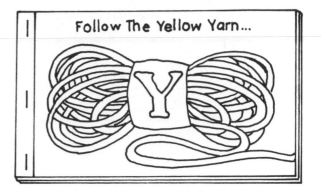

Follow The Yellow Yarn...

Haircuts For The Woolseys
by Tomie dePaola

- In this story, the word *fleece* is used to describe the warm Woolsey coats. Have your youngsters think of more names that might be used for fleece such as *fur, hair,* or *wool.* Have them brainstorm a list of adjectives that describe the Woolseys' coats. Have them describe how the Woolsey children looked before and after their haircuts.

- When the cold snap hit, the Woolsey family used several means to get warm again. Ask your youngsters to tell you what each Woolsey adult did to warm up the house. Ask them to tell you what they do to get warm on a cold day.

- Granny Woolsey saved the day with the warm wool sweaters that she knitted for the lambs. Help your youngsters list the steps needed to make fleece into yarn and yarn into sweaters. Follow up the discussion with each student sharing his completed yarn booklet page on page 174.

Books About Yarn

Charlie Needs A Cloak by Tomie dePaola
Derek The Knitting Dinosaur by Mary Blackwood
The Mitten: A Ukrainian Folktale by Jan Brett
Mrs. McDockerty's Knitting by Ruth Martinez

More Yarn and *Y* Activities

- Decorate a large paper *Y* with lengths of different colored yarn.

- Ask your local toy store to recommend a yo-yo expert to come and demonstrate this classic toy for your students. Bring in some yo-yos for the students to experiment with.

- Find a picture of a yak. Explain to the children that a yak is a black, shaggy animal with a shoulder height of about 5'2". They are found in central Asia and northern China. Their long shaggy hair is used to make rope, the meat is eaten, and the milk is used for drinking and making butter.

- Play a recording of a person yodeling and let your students try to reproduce the sounds. Record your students' attempts and play it back for them.

- Make large *Y*s on paper by giving the children short lengths of fat, yellow, craft yarn and have them glue *Y* shapes to construction paper.

- Serve a yummy *Y* snack of small cups of flavored yogurt.

Booklet page

Use with "Yarn Booklet Page" on page 172 and the third *Haircuts For The Woolseys* activity on page 173.

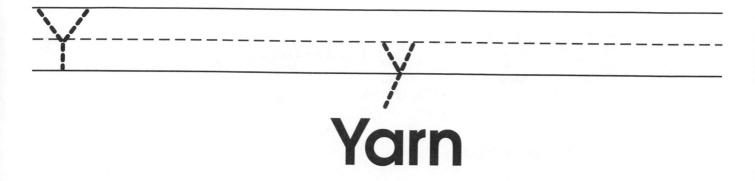

Yarn

Here are my favorite colors of yarn.

They will make a

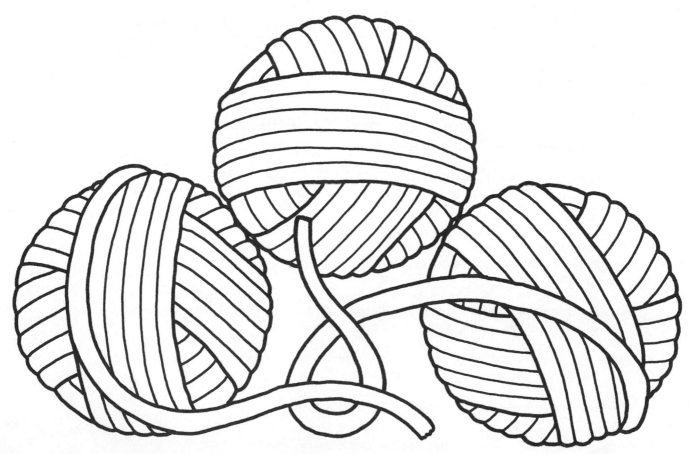

yak

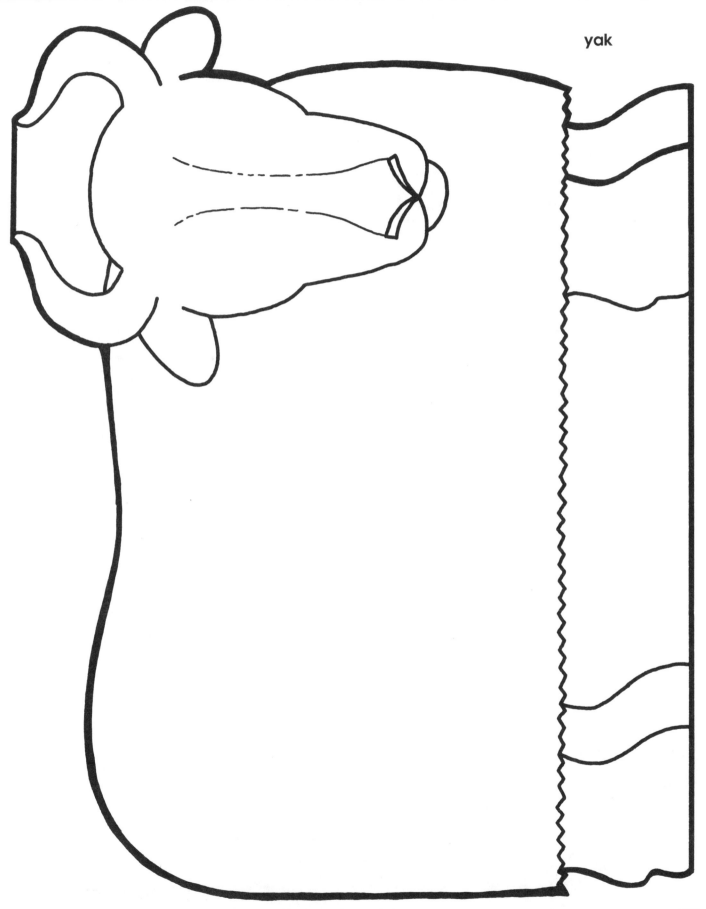

Follow The Yellow Yarn...

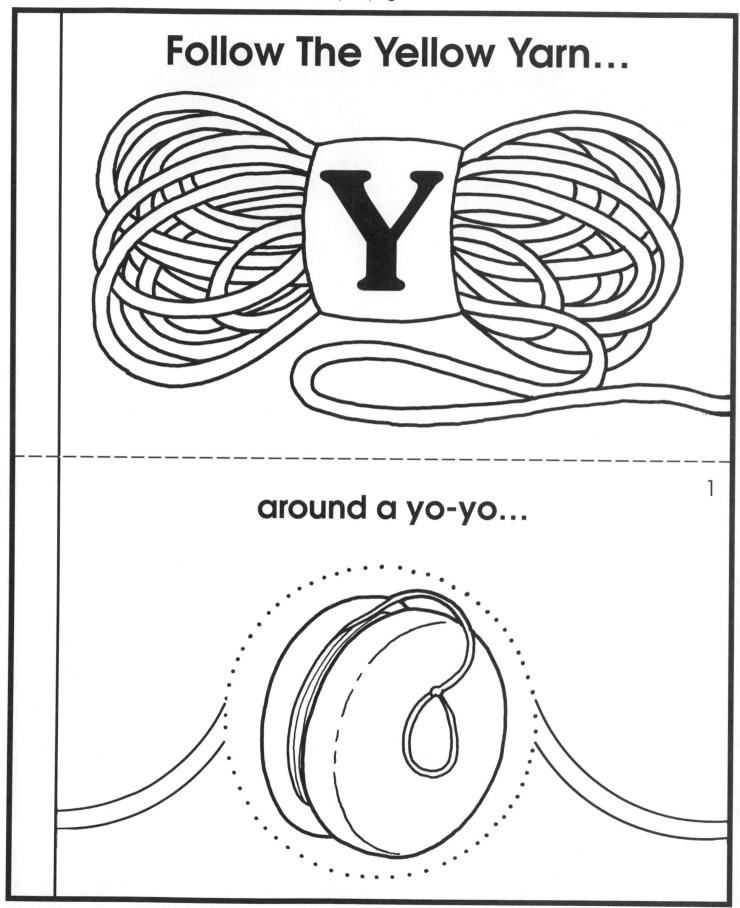

around a yo-yo...

1

2

over a yawn...

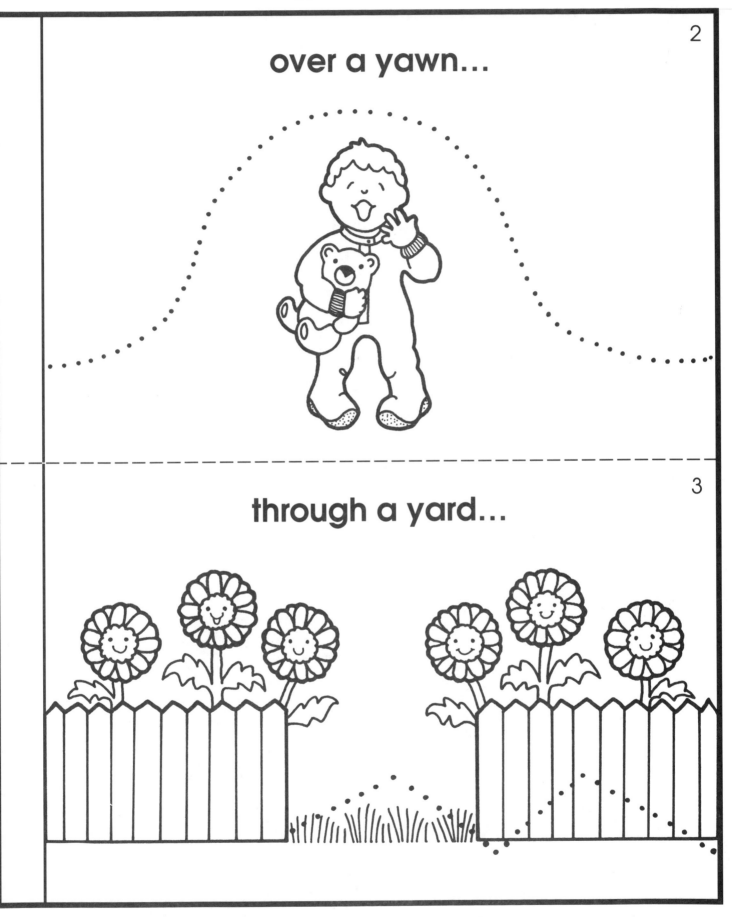

3

through a yard...

4

under a yak...

5

and on you!

Z is for zoo

Z will be the last, but not the least, of your alphabet accomplishments.

Zoo Poem

Pass around a stuffed zebra as you read this fun poem aloud.

1. One day I went
    To the Zebra Zoo
    To see a zebra show.

2. The zebras wore
    Such funny suits—
    Just black and white, you know.

3. The zebras' legs
    Were black and white.
    Their "stripey" tails were, too.

4. I'd like to wear
    A zebra suit
    To see the Zebra Zoo.

A Z Recipe

Divide the contents of several boxes of animal cookies onto paper plates according to animal species. Put the hippo cookies on one plate, the lion cookies on another plate, and so on. Make a vocabulary card for each type of animal and staple it to the paper plate. Make a large sign labeled "Zany Snack Zoo." Place the sign and the labeled plates on a table. Have your youngsters choose cookies from this zoo buffet for a snack. Serve the cookies with zoo juice (any juice of your choice).

"Animals Live In The Zoo"

Sing this song to the tune of "Mary Had A Little Lamb."

> Animals live in the zoo,
> In the zoo, in the zoo.
> Animals live in the zoo.
> Let's go there and see some!
>
> [Elephants] live in the zoo,
> In the zoo, in the zoo.
> [Elephants] live in the zoo.
> Let's go there and see some!

Each time you repeat the verse, use another animal in the song. Include *crocodiles, chimpanzees, polar bears,* and *kangaroos.*

Zoo Booklet Page

Use the *Z* booklet page on page 181 as directed for previous letters. Have each youngster draw an animal under the archway. Write each child's dictation in the space provided to complete the sentence starter.

Zippy Zebras

Give your classroom a little zest with these bulletin-board zebras. Reproduce the patterns on pages 182 and 183 on white construction paper. Have each youngster use a black crayon to color stripes on the zebra's body, tail, and ear pieces. Have youngsters color the mane black. Let them choose any bright color to color the large *Z.* Cut out all of the pieces. Glue the two body pieces together where indicated. Glue the mane and ear to the zebra's head. Glue on a wiggle eye. Attach the tail to the zebra with a brad. Glue the *Z* to the zebra's body. Post these on a bulletin board titled "Zippy Zebras."

Zoo Tachistoscope

Let your youngsters take a trip to the zoo for some hands-on learning fun. Reproduce the zoo, picture strips, and *Z* block patterns on pages 184 and 185 on white construction paper. Color and cut them out. Slit along the dotted lines on the zoo piece. Glue the *Z* blocks to the zoo piece where indicated. Glue the picture strips together; then thread the strip through the slits where indicated on the zoo picture. Pull the strip to reveal a *Z* picture and/or word.

Zoo Song
by Barbara Bottner

- Have your youngsters discuss why the three zoo animals were singing, playing, and dancing. Have students decide what a zoo animal usually does all day in a zoo. Have them compare the benefits and drawbacks of living in the wild to the benefits and drawbacks of living in a zoo.

- The animals in this zoo lived in boring cages. Have your youngsters discuss and list ideas for zoo animal enclosures that would be interesting for the animals. Have each youngster draw an interesting zoo habitat for a favorite zoo animal.

- One page in the story shows several other animals listening to the three animal performers. Ask your youngsters to name these animals. Have them add more animals to the zoo list and then imagine what each one's performing talents might be!

Zoo Stories

A New True Book—Zoos by Karen Jacobsen
One, Two, Three To The Zoo by Eric Carle
A Visit To The Zoo by Sylvia R. Tester
Where Will The Animals Stay? by Stephanie Calmenson
A Zoo In Our House by Heather Eyles

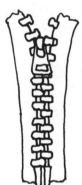

More Zoo And *Z* Activities

- Introduce your students to onomatopoeia by having them imitate the sounds for the words *zip, zoom,* and *zing.* Have the children name items that would make these sounds.

- Have a zipper day and encourage your children to wear clothing that has a zipper. Count the total number of zippers in your classroom and then create a graph to show how many students have zippers on shirts, pants, jackets, sweaters, or have no zipper.

- Display copies of zoo magazines and books in your classroom.

- Discuss what kinds of animals are zoo animals. Collect pictures of several animals and have your students identify if they are zoo animals, farm animals, circus animals, or pet animals. Sort the pictures into labeled categories.

- Show the children how to make a zigzag pattern. Have them draw zigzag designs on a piece of construction paper and color them.

- Cut a large zero out of construction paper and introduce the number to the children. Explain that we use the numeral zero to represent none. Have the children demonstrate by holding up zero fingers.

- Serve zwieback toast to the children for a quick *Z* snack.

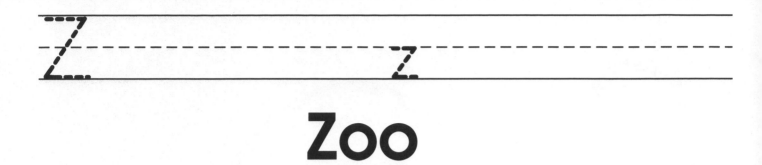

Zoo

We went to the zoo.

We saw a

Patterns
Use with the "Zippy Zebras" activity on page 179.

ear

zebra front

mane

Glue to back of zebra's head and neck here.

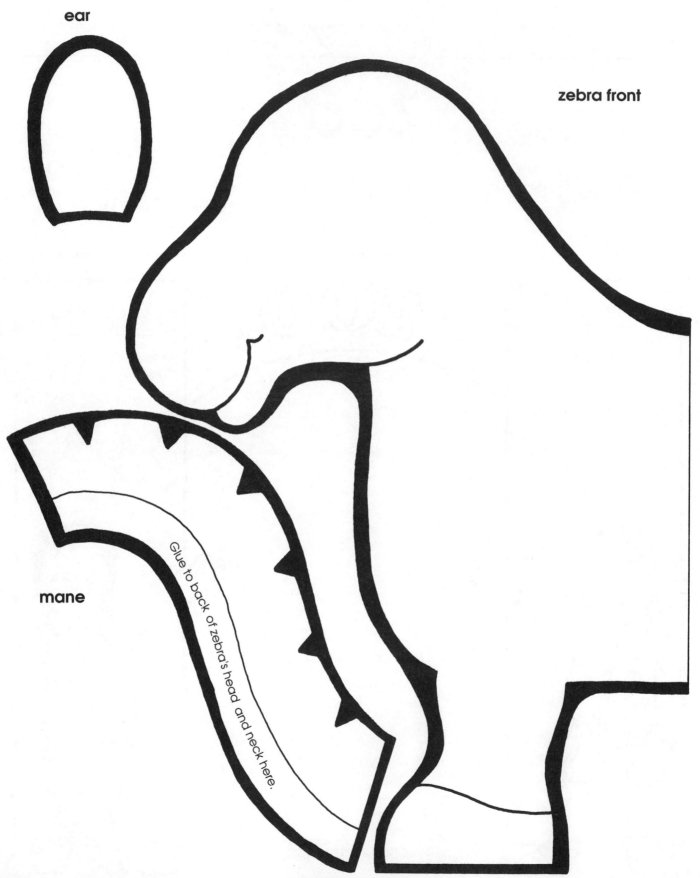

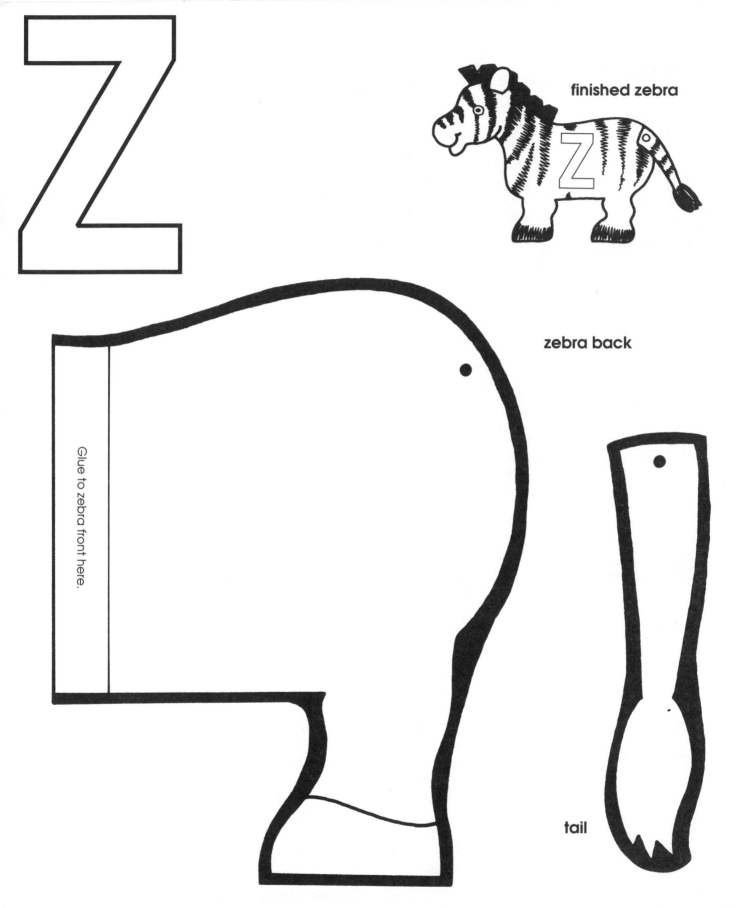

finished zebra

zebra back

Glue to zebra front here.

tail

Pattern

Use with the "Zoo Tachistoscope" activity on page 180.

zoo piece

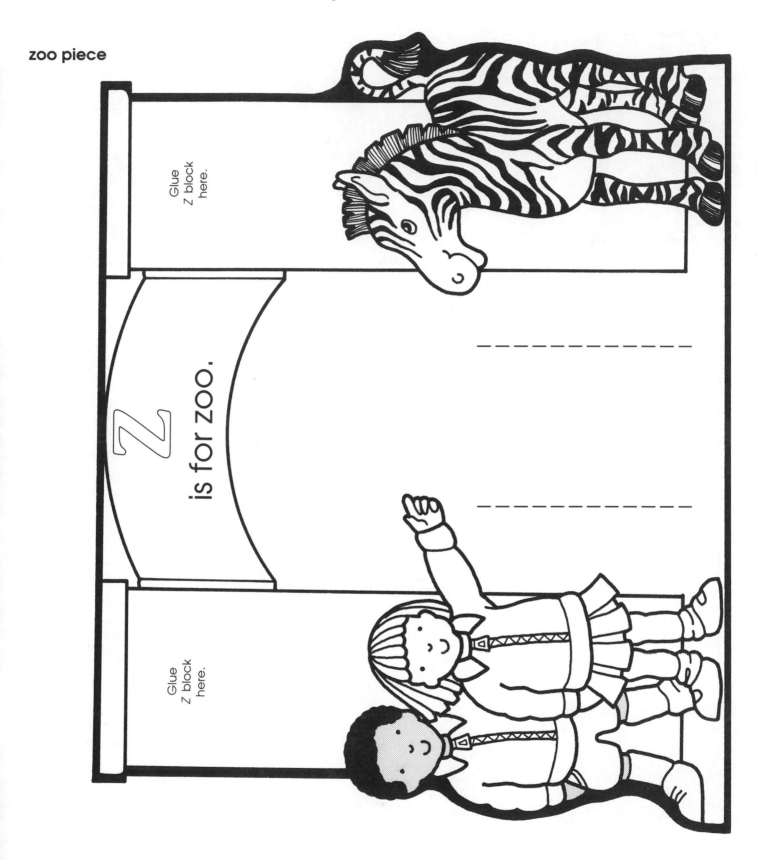

Glue Z block here.

Z

is for zoo.

Glue Z block here.

_ _ _ _ _ _ _ _ _ _ _

_ _ _ _ _ _ _ _ _ _ _

Z blocks

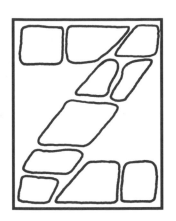

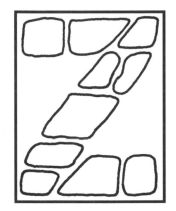

picture strips

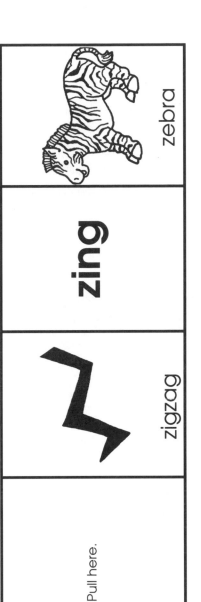

zebra

zing

zigzag

Pull here.

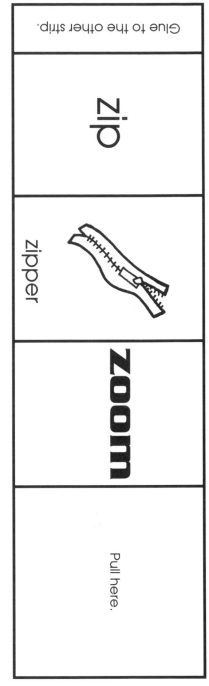

Glue to the other strip.

zip

zipper

zoom

Pull here.

Additional Alphabet Books

- *ABC Bunny* by Wanda Gág
- *A B See!* by Tana Hoban
- *Alligator Arrived With Apples: A Potluck Alphabet Feast* by Crescent Dragonwagon
- *Alphabetics* by Suse MacDonald
- *Alphabears* by Kathleen Hague
- *Alphabet Puzzle* by Jill Downie
- *Anno's Alphabet: An Adventure In Imagination* by Mitsumasa Anno
- *Antler, Bear, Canoe: A Northwoods Alphabet Year* by Betsy Bowen
- *Ape In A Cape: An Alphabet Of Odd Animals* by Fritz Eichenberg
- *A Caribou Alphabet* by Mary Beth Owens
- *Chicka Chicka Boom Boom* by Bill Martin, Jr., and John Archambault
- *Eating The Alphabet: Fruits And Vegetables From A To Z* by Lois Ehlert
- *Ed Emberley's ABC* by Ed Emberley
- *I Spy—An Alphabet In Art* by Lucy Micklethwait
- *I Unpacked My Grandmother's Trunk: A Picture Book Game* by Susan Ramsay Hoguet
- *On Market Street* by Arnold Lobel
- *Quentin Blake's ABC* by Quentin Blake
- *The Z Was Zapped* by Chris Van Allsburg

Award

Congratulations!

_____
student's name

has worked hard to
learn all the letters
of the alphabet and
their sounds.

_____
date

_____
teacher's name

My Alphabet Book

By

_____

- -

_____